M000295895

WHEN WASHINGTON BURNED

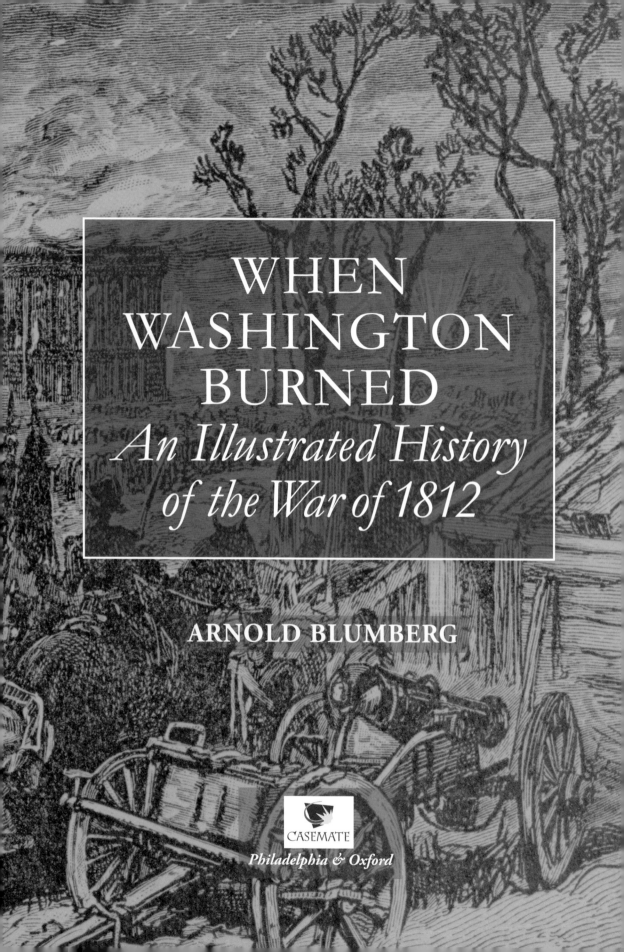

WHEN WASHINGTON BURNED

An Illustrated History of the War of 1812

ARNOLD BLUMBERG

CASEMATE

Philadelphia & Oxford

Published in the United States of America and Great Britain in 2012 by
CASEMATE PUBLISHERS
908 Darby Road, Havertown, PA 19083
and
10 Hythe Bridge Street, Oxford, OX1 2EW

Copyright 2012 © Casemate Publishers

ISBN 978-1-61200-101-2
Digital Edition: ISBN 978-1-61200-113-5

Cataloging-in-publication data is available from the Library of Congress
and the British Library.

All rights reserved. No part of this book may be reproduced or transmitted in any form or by any means,
electronic or mechanical including photocopying, recording or by any information storage and retrieval
system, without permission from the Publisher in writing.

10 9 8 7 6 5 4 3 2 1

Printed and bound in the United States of America.

For a complete list of Casemate titles please contact:

CASEMATE PUBLISHERS (US)
Telephone (610) 853-9131, Fax (610) 853-9146
E-mail: casemate@casematepublishing.com

CASEMATE PUBLISHERS (UK)
Telephone (01865) 241249, Fax (01865) 794449
E-mail: casemate-uk@casematepublishing.co.uk

Image, title page: *Capture and Burning of Washington by the British in 1814.*
   Courtesy of the Library of Congress

Unless otherwise noted, all images courtesy of Peter Newark's Pictures.

Contents

Dedication

To my wife Marsha, who has happily supported my interest in the study of military history these many years, I lovingly dedicate this book.

Acknowledgments

———◆◆◆———

I WOULD LIKE TO THANK THE PEOPLE WHOSE AID AND SUPPORT MADE THIS BOOK possible. First, I wish to thank Tim Newark, author, historian, and editor. His expert and insightful advice about what ingredients make for an interesting and informative historical narrative guided my writing.

To Sandra Jackson, Supervisor of the Interlibrary Loan Department, the Milton S. Eisenhower Library, John Hopkins University in Baltimore, Maryland, I want to thank for her courtesy, kindness, and timely responses to my requests for material. Her able assistants, Jeanette Brown and Jeff Dysart, not only made me feel at home but also took an interest in my project, which greatly encouraged my effort.

To Casemate Publishers, I would like to extend my gratitude for their confidence in me to put a manuscript together, and their desire to add to the material on the War of 1812 in its 200th anniversary year. The fine illustrations they have included in the work add greatly to the volume.

To my daughters, Beth and Maureen, whose encouragement helped me carry on, thank you for taking the time and interest in your old Dad's avocation. To my wife Marsha, thanks for the occasional needed push to get the job done.

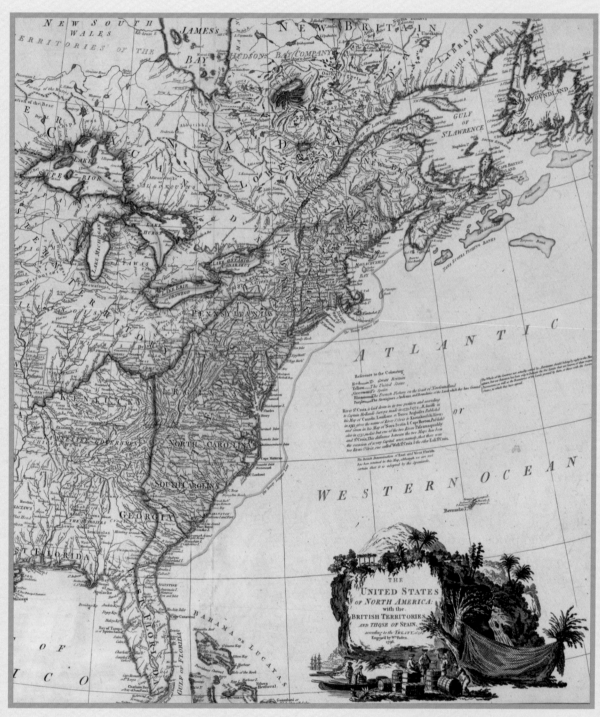

Map of the United States with the British Territories and those of Spain according
to the treaty of 1784. Engraved by William Faden (1750–1836).
Courtesy of the Library and Archives of Canada (NMC24667)

Introduction

It has been called the "forgotten conflict," "the unnecessary war," and the "obscure war," all appropriate appellations for the early 19th century military struggle—the War of 1812—fought between the British Empire and the United States of America. Initiated by unclear causes, and ending with equally murky consequences, it is a stretch to claim it was a US victory, or a great British triumph. Concluded in 1815 with an agreement acknowledging the pre-war status quo, modern historians of both countries continue to question why it was even fought in the first instance.

Marked by domestic opposition, from the Federalists in the United States and much of the merchant class in England, and relegated by the British to the status of a mere colonial disruption due to her ongoing war with Napoleonic France, the American War was perceived by the world as a sorry little side show. And yet, despite this criticism, the conflict did produce genuine martial heroes: Andrew Jackson, Jacob Brown, and Winfield Scott for the Americans, and Isaac Brock and Gordon Drummond for the British, not to forget the honorable Shawnee Indian Tecumseh. While the standing of the British Army was not diminished by the struggle, that of the American Army rose, from amateurs in arms to a potentially respectable fighting force led by promising officers. The United States Navy came away from the combat with a brilliant record written by its frigates. Indeed, it was from this increasing military prowess on land and at sea that the United States was able to secure its status as a formidable power in the years after 1815, and expand its international influence and prosperity both at home and abroad. For the British, although they gained no new territory, they were able to keep Canada, which was their primary objective during the war.

It is not the purpose of this book to describe all the myriad military events that took place during the War of 1812. Instead, this book highlights the major campaigns and battles and points out the key military figures that contributed to the outcome of the war. As such, I have not mentioned certain episodes such as the Patriot War in East Florida, or the activities in the West after 1813, since they did not involve significant American or British forces; nor are the many small-scale raids and retaliatory actions that took place in all theaters included. The same can be said for the American and British general officers mentioned in the book. From the incompetent to the very capable, they all deserve to be more fully described, since they were genuine products of their time and reflected how 19th century warfare was waged. Hopefully, in its 200th anniversary year, the reader will find interest in the military events and the soldiers who took part in them, and agree that the War of 1812, fought by American, British, and Indian fighting men should not be considered a forgotten war.

CHAPTER ONE

The Road to War

—◦◦◦—

"PREPARE FOR WAR" WAS THE CLARION CALL OF THE FEDERALIST PARTY. NEITHER the Federalists nor the Republicans differed over the wider objectives of American national policy during the late 18th and early 19th centuries. Both political parties agreed that the highest national objectives should be economic prosperity at home while protecting the nation's rights and maintaining its neutrality abroad. What divided these political factions was the best way to achieve those ends during the series of conflicts that marked the period from 1793 to 1815.

"War is a great calamity," said Federalist Connecticut US Congressman Benjamin Tallmadge, "and the surest way to avoid it, is to be prepared for it." As a result, the Federalists put in place a program of financial and military preparedness in the 1790s. Closely aligned with fiscal reforms, the Federalists expanded the nation's armed forces. The standing peacetime army was increased from 840 officers and enlisted men in 1789, to 5,400 personnel by 1801. The latter year saw the navy, which had been completely dismantled at the conclusion of the American War of Independence, provided with 13 frigates in service as well as six ships-of-the-line under various stages of construction. Rounding out their defense measures, the Federalists allotted over $1 million for the protection of port cities from attack from the sea.

In the diplomatic field, the Federalists hoped to bolster national defense by advancing a pro-British foreign policy. They surmised that British naval power was both a potential threat and a shield to American trade. To neutralize the former and take advantage of the latter they pushed through Congress the Jay Treaty of 1794, an Anglo-American agreement that regulated commerce between the two nations as well as defined the rights of neutrals in time of war. The treaty stimulated an explosion of US export trade from $33 million in the year it was signed, to $94 million by 1801. An additional benefit derived from the treaty was that America gained a cordial relationship with the only European power that could menace its shores and seaborne commerce.

Despite the real prosperity Federalist policies had garnered, the party met a decisive defeat in the national election of 1800. Heavy taxation, resulting in a large national debt to support the country's defense, the public's fear of a permanent military establishment, an attempt to silence political opposition through anti-sedition legislation, a pro-British foreign policy— which alienated many Americans who still felt the effects of the revolt against the mother country—doomed the Federalists and their programs at the polls.

With their victory in the election of 1800, the Republican Party, under the new President Thomas Jefferson, was determined to reverse the Federalist agenda that had been in place for the past decade. All the Federalist economic policies, such as internal taxes and infrastructure spending, were rolled back in the name of economizing and paying down the national debt.

The national defense establishment did not escape the new cost cutting measures either. The peacetime army was reduced in 1802 from 5,400 to 3,300 officers and enlisted

Thomas Jefferson, 3rd President of the United States, 1801–09. During his administration, tensions rose between the US and Britain. Portrait by Rembrandt Peale.

men. The result was a severe lack of training for the men and an almost nonexistent level of professionalism in the officer corps. Senior officer slots were filled with Republican political appointees with no military schooling, their only qualification being that they were loyal to the Republican Party. General Winfield Scott observed that most were "imbeciles and ignoramuses." By 1810, the incompetence of the army's top brass was so evident and demoralizing to the rank and file soldier that one Republican politician, Nathaniel Macon, opined that "The state of that Army is enough to make any man who has the smallest love of country wish to get rid of it."

The navy got no better treatment from the Republicans. Their mantra, according to Republican Samuel McKee, was that a nation with a navy was a nation constantly engaged in war. To prevent that, and with an eye toward limiting government expenditures, construction of all capital ships was halted, and only seven frigates were retained in service. In lieu of a viable navy, the Republican government spent $2.8 million between 1801 and 1812 on coastal defense installations. But without a reasonably sized mobile fleet, the cities of the eastern seaboard remained exposed to enemy warships and amphibious forces.

Distrustful of a standing army and navy, fearing that these fostered special interest groups that presented a danger to government, the Jefferson administration felt the need to gut the nation's defense establishment. In its opinion the most reliable and patriotic defenders of the country would not be expensive and permanently maintained regular soldiers and sailors, but state militia serving on land, and privateers on the ocean. Besides, both being democratic in character, they would pose no threat to government institutions. Equally important, they were cheap, not having to be paid until called to service, with monetary outlays ceasing when they were no longer required. The fact that, on the whole, the militia was ill-trained, poorly equipped, and miserably led, while privateers could not fight enemy warships, break hostile blockades, or protect friendly coastal centers, seemed not to concern Republican leaders. What did matter most to them was economic retrenchment, the basic Republican Party political tenet that got them into office, and in their minds, would keep them there.

❖　❖　❖

The war between Great Britain and Napoleonic France resumed at the end of the 1801–1803 Peace of Amiens. During that short-lived truce, America's trade advantages dropped by almost one half. The resumption of conflict between the two Great Powers saw American overseas commerce climb as she again became one of the largest carriers of goods between the western hemisphere and Europe. Britain's remarkable indulgence toward the increasing US-Atlantic trade dominance prompted James Monroe, the American minister to London, to report to his government in 1804 that: "The truth is that our commerce never enjoyed in any war, as much freedom, and indeed favor from this govt [British] as it now does." However, by October of the next year, Monroe was complaining that the British were attempting "to subject our commerce at present and hereafter to every restraint in their power." What had changed Britain's attitude toward American trade practices since Monroe's initial remarks of 1804?

British authorities had become increasingly alarmed at what they detected as unfair, even fraudulent, American trade activities and had started to strictly enforce Great Britain's maritime doctrine known as the Rule of 1756. The Rule stated that trade closed to a neutral nation in time of peace could not be opened in time of war. Its purpose was to prevent US merchants from freighting goods between France and her West Indian colonies when French vessels could not get to sea. But American shippers were able to get around the Rule by first stopping at an American port prior to continuing to or from the French West Indies, thus transforming direct trade between France and her overseas possessions into a triangular one.

Determined both to regulate and grab a share of the lucrative trade the US was reaping through the French-West Indies commercial traffic, the British declared that they would no longer allow the American practice of funneling goods through US ports as a way to evade the Rule of 1756. Soon Britain began seizing American merchant craft engaged in the re-export business, resulting in crippling financial losses to Yankee ocean commerce. British interference continued through mid-1806 until it was discontinued, but the harm to American commercial interests had been done, and the resentment by the Americans toward their British cousins did not abate.

Along with the issue of the rights of neutrals to freely trade during wartime, impressments—the British practice of taking American seaman by force, claiming they were British subjects, from American ships on the high seas—caused great bitterness and friction between the two nations. During the period 1803–1812, some 6,000 American citizens were forced into British service as a result of impressment. This practice was deemed essential by Britain as the only way to maintain crew strength in the Royal Navy during its life-and-death struggle with France.

In addition to the questions of rights of neutrals to trade, and impressment, America and Great Britain argued over several other maritime issues: British methods of imposing internationally recognized blockades; the definition of what was contraband that could be seized by a belligerent from a neutral; and the common practice of British warships violating American territorial waters.

In an attempt to resolve many of these differences, Great Britain and the United States forged an agreement—the Monroe-Pinkney Treaty of 1806—that went a long way toward satisfying American concerns about securing their commercial rights. But President Jefferson considered the British commitments in the treaty minor, and since it did not include a British promise to end impressment completely, he refused to send the treaty to the US Senate for ratification. His inaction resulted in a further strain of American-British relations.

✦ ✦ ✦

The period after the rejection of the Monroe-Pinkney Treaty witnessed a rapid deterioration of American-British relations. The first critical episode in that downward spiral came

Impressment was one of the causes of the War of 1812. Here, American sailors are forcibly taken from the USS Chesapeake following a clash with the British frigate HMS Leopard in 1807.

in the form of the *Chesapeake* affair. On June 22, 1807, the American frigate USS *Chesapeake,* sailing for the Mediterranean Sea and completely unprepared for combat, was attacked by HMS *Leopard.* The latter's intent was to capture British deserters assumed to be on board the American ship. The scheme was initiated despite the fact that the Royal Navy did not claim the right to search for or impress men on neutral warships. When the American commander refused to allow the British to board and search his craft, the *Leopard* opened fire, killing three and wounding 18 others. Devastated by the assault, the US ship struck her colors and permitted the British to remove the alleged deserters. Despite an offer of reparations by Britain, and a return of those sailors taken from the *Chesapeake,* the controversy dragged on until 1811 and continued to contribute to the growing animosity between the United States and His Britannic Majesty's government.

Hard on the heels of the *Chesapeake* affair, another act by the British surfaced to complicate the already strained relations between the American Republic and British Empire. British Orders in Council—a series of dictates issued throughout 1807 designed to counter Napoleon's Berlin Decree of 1806—came into affect. The French declaration proclaimed that the British Isles were to be in a state of isolation by land and sea. The decree prohibited all commerce with British ports, while goods from either British or her colonial ports were subject to seizure. In response, the Orders in Council banned trade from ports controlled by Britain's enemies. Later, they compelled all neutral shipping to

By the Virtue, Firmness and Patriotism of

JEFFERSON & MADISON,

Our Difficulties with England are settled—our Ships have been preserved, and our Seamen will, hereafter, be respected
while sailing under our National Flag.

NEW-YORK, SATURDAY MORNING, APRIL 22, 1809.

IMPORTANT.

By the President of the United States.—A Proclamation.

WHEREAS it is provided by the 11th section of the act of Congress, entitled "An
"act to interdict the commercial intercourse between the United States and Great Bri-
"tain and France, and their dependencies; and for other purposes,"—and that "in
"case either France or Great Britain shall so revoke or modify her edicts as that they,
"shall cease to violate the neutral commerce of the United States," the President is au-
thorised to declare the same by proclamation, after which the trade suspended by the said
act and by an act laying an Embargo, on all ships and vessels in the ports and harbours of
the United States and the several acts supplementary thereto may be renewed with the
nation so doing. And whereas the Honourable David Montague Erskine, his Britannic
Majesty's Envoy Extraordinary and Minister Plenipotentiary, has by the order and in the
name of his sovereign declared to this Government, that the British Orders in Council
of January and November, 1807, will have been withdrawn, as respects the United
States on the 10th day of June next. Now therefore I James Madison, President of
the United States, do hereby proclaim that the orders in council aforesaid will have
been withdrawn on the tenth day of June next; after which day the trade of the United
States with Great Britain, as suspended by the act of Congress above mentioned, and
an act laying an embargo on all ships and vessels in the ports and harbors of the United
States, and the several acts supplementary thereto, may be renewed.

Given under my hand and the seal of the United States, at Washington, the nineteenth day of April, in the year of our Lord, one
(L. s)   thousand eight hundred and nine, and of the Independence
of the United States, the thirty-third.
                                          JAMES MADISON.

By the President,
RT. SMITH, *Secretary of State.*

Republican broadside published in 1809, claiming that Britain would respect sailors and ships sailing under the American flag.

stop at British harbors to be searched, and where they were subject to capture and confis-
cation. In addition, they required all neutral merchants to pay duties and apply for licenses
issued by Britain in order to carry on trade with the Continent.

Responding to the Orders, France promulgated the Milan Decree in December
1807, extending to neutrals the embargo on products destined for Great Britain. American
trade was thus caught in a vice formed by British and French trade restrictions. The cost
to the young nation in lost shipping was significant. Between 1803 and 1807, 528 Ameri-
can-flagged ships were seized by the British and 206 by the French.

President Jefferson and Congress, in a flawed attempt to strike back at Britain,
declared an embargo prohibiting all US ships from trading with Europe, and banned the
importation of goods manufactured in England. This plan to get the British to relax her
trade controls on neutral shipping was unsuccessful and caused more economic suffering

James Madison, 4th President of the United States from 1809 and during the War of 1812. Portrait by Gilbert Stuart.

in the United States than to its intended target. The Embargo Act of 1807 drove the nation into a severe depression as exports dropped from $108 million in 1807 to $22 million in 1808, which resulted in 55,000 seamen and 100,000 other workers thrown out of work.

In 1809, the Republican James Madison became President. In that same year, the United States Congress replaced the failed Embargo Act with the Non-Intercourse Act which reopened trade with all nations except Britain and France, but, like the Embargo Act, it did not gain concessions from the two belligerents. Britain issued additional Orders in Council in 1809 that further injured American trade. In 1810, Napoleon offered to lift French restrictions on American shipping if the British would abolish their series of Orders in Council. Instead, London in 1811 issued new edicts that curtailed the Yankees' ability to trade with the West Indies, and placed heavy levies on all goods entering the United States.

✦   ✦   ✦

As the non-importation law continued to degrade US-British relations, events in 1811 moved the countries closer to war. The first involved the *Little Belt* Incident—in essence the *Chesapeake* affair in reverse. On May 16, the large American frigate USS *President* clashed with the much smaller British sloop HMS *Little Belt*. The resulting gunfight left nine killed and 23 wounded among the British crew. An outraged British public called for revenge, even if it meant war. "The blood of our murdered countrymen must be avenged," said the *London Courier* newspaper. "The conduct of America leaves us no alternative." On the other hand, the Americans felt that the stain on their national honor caused by the attack on the *Chesapeake* four years earlier had been properly wiped clean.

As the *Little Belt* affair pushed the two nations closer to war, America's attention was diverted from maritime disputes with Great Britain to her security and territorial expansion interests in the Old Northwest (now including Ohio, Michigan and Indiana). Around the heavily forested Great Lakes, about 50,000 Native Americans occupied the land as the Americans relentlessly pushed their settlements into the area. The Indians relied on the British in Canada to help them resist the American encroachment by supplying them with weapons, while the British counted on the natives to aid them in defending Canada in event of war with the United States. "The British cannot hold Upper Canada without the assistance of the Indians," concluded Michigan's governor William Hull in March 1811, but the "Indians cannot conduct a war without the assistance of a civilized nation."

Although the British counseled restraint to their Indian allies, the United States regarded the Indians as pawns in an insidious British plot to ravage the frontier. While the British viewed the natives as autonomous peoples dwelling between the British Empire and the American Republic, and therefore free to make their own alliances, the American view was that the Native Americans should be US dependents, living within a fixed boundary separating British from American sovereignty. Furthermore, the Jefferson administration had hoped to absorb the Indians into American society by transforming them from hunter-gatherers to farmers without tribal identities.

This transformation would not only wean the Indians from their reliance on martial aid from the British, but also make it easier for American settlers to obtain Indian lands, since sedentary Indian farmers would need far less land than roaming hunters. On Jefferson's orders, the territorial governors of Indiana and Michigan had pressured the tribesmen to secede millions of acres for mere pennies each. William Henry Harrison of Indiana was especially relentless in this regard. His negotiations of land cession agreements with chiefs of minor tribes, without getting approval for the sale from all the Indian leaders as required, was an open breach of prior US-Indian treaties. The result was outraged young native warriors who sought redress for their grievances against the United States through force of arms.

They turned for leadership to the charismatic Shawnee warrior Tecumseh—also known as "Shooting Star"—renowned for his statesmanship and moderation. While the 44-year-old Tecumseh worked to forge bonds of unity among the Indians of the Old

Northwest, his brother, Tenskwatawa ("the Prophet"), became the spiritual head of the growing Indian coalition—an Indian confederacy Tecumseh hoped would stretch from the Great Lakes to the Gulf of Mexico, forming a buffer state between Canada and the eastern United States.

Tecumseh and Tenskwatawa met Harrison in August 1810 to lodge a complaint about the blatantly illegal land transactions Harrison had conducted with the Indians. This meeting, and further complaints, produced no results. Rejecting Harrison's treaties, the brothers vowed armed resistance and gathered 1,000 warriors at their main village of Prophetstown, also known as Tippecanoe, in the Wabash Valley of northern Indiana. In November 1811, Harrison marched against them with 1,000 US regular soldiers and volunteer frontiersmen. The US army made camp about two miles from the village. On November 7, it was attacked on orders from the Prophet in a surprise assault by 600 Indian braves. Tecumseh was not at Prophetstown at the time, having travelled to consult with other tribes further south.

The battle of Tippecanoe turned into a vicious hand-to-hand affair that mauled

James Monroe, Secretary of State during the Madison administration, later 5th President of the United States.

Harrison's force and cost it 68 killed and 126 wounded, but ultimately proved an American victory. The Indians, losing about 100 warriors in the fight, abandoned Prophetstown, which was burned by the Americans. Harrison then led his command back to its base at Vincennes. On his return from the south, Tecumseh gathered the remnants of his followers and joined the British at Amherstburg.

The battle had destroyed the nucleus of Tecumseh's nascent Indian confederacy but did not stop Indian depredations on the frontier. The Indians, with aid from the British, continued to raid over the following winter and spring. An editorial in the *Lexington Reporter* expressed the general sentiment of the frontier: "The British are the principal [force]— the Indians only hired assassins." Politicians in Washington pointed to unrest on the border as another example of British duplicity and the grave danger it presented to the population of the trans-Appalachian west, thundering that it could only be extinguished by going to war with Britain.

American territorial ambitions were not confined to the Northwest. Jefferson had claimed all through his Presidency that Spanish West Florida had been part of the Louisiana Purchase, a proposition denied by France. A US-inspired revolution in September 1810 saw the brief occupation of West Florida. US troops took over Spanish East Florida in

Tecumseh, chief of the Shawnee tribe, allied himself with the British against the Americans. Portrayed here wearing a British tunic and medal.

March of 1812 and left troops in the area even after President Madison, in April of that year, denied any responsibility for the incursion. Notwithstanding the President's denial in the affair, the expanding young nation would soon turn its eyes once more to Florida.

✦ ✦ ✦

Apart from maritime issues, such as the rights of neutrals and impressment, the Indian problem and the quest for new land, America's most significant impetus for war seems to have been voiced by William Cobbett. An English journalist and political reformer, Cobbett had resided in Philadelphia from 1793 to 1800 and had become a good judge of the American character. In his opinion, the real cause for the outbreak of war between America and Britain was that, "There seemed to be wanting just such a war as this to complete the separation of England from America; and to make the latter feel that she had no safety against the former but in the arms of her free citizens."

In other words, according to Cobbett, the War of 1812 would assure the legacy and results of the War of American Independence by revealing to the world that the United States was free, independent, self-reliant, capable, and a power to be reckoned with among the nations.

Tenskwatawa, also known as "the Prophet," was the brother of Tecumseh, and spiritual head of the Indian coalition against the Americans.

In 1810, Chief Tecumseh defies William Henry Harrison, Governor of Indiana Territory, and declares he will seek an alliance with the British.

Contemporary cartoon depicting a disloyal Federalist editor failing to impress three American sailors not to go to war against Britain.

The Twelfth Congress, known to history as the War Congress, convened on November 4, 1811. Although the Republicans held commanding majorities in the United States House of Representatives and Senate, they lacked effective leadership and were racked by factionalism. This condition was dramatically transformed by the presence of a new group of 11 young Republicans called the War Hawks. Under their leader, Henry Clay from Kentucky, key House committees were packed with War Hawks or their supporters, and House rules were interpreted in order to advance their pro-war movement. The War Hawks brought the backbenchers—mostly Republicans—in both the House and Senate on board in support of their desire for a war with Great Britain, to finally resolve the tensions that had plagued America over the previous ten years.

The final decision for war was not taken up until June 1812, but major congressional proposals for preparation for conflict were passed earlier that year. They included expanding the Regular Army to 35,000 recruits, raising a 50,000 man volunteer force, refitting warships, arming all merchant vessels, and appropriating $500,000 for coastal defense. To finance the coming struggle, the government was authorized to borrow $11 million, though any taxes needed to support the conflict would not be raised until war had been declared.

On June 18, 1812, President James Madison signed the war bill. It passed the Senate by a vote of 19 to 13, and in the House 79 to 49. Hostilities between the United States of America and Great Britain had officially begun. It is quite possible that the measure was intended merely to wring concessions from the British, not start a full-blown conflict. The American government knew of the fight for survival the British were engaged in with Napoleon, as well as the vulnerability of Canada to an American invasion. The Madison administration appeared to be using the declaration of war as a negotiating tool when the President and his Secretary of State, James Monroe, laid out the American terms for peace to the British shortly after war was declared.

The British government was on notice of American preparations for war, but London, in the words of the Lord Castlereagh, British Foreign Secretary, viewed these acts of "belligerence in the United States as to be no more than party maneuvering." But, as the middle of 1812 approached, the British became more alarmed at America's militaristic determination, and, in an effort to appease their former colonies repealed their Orders in Council on June 21.

News of the American declaration of war reached Great Britain on July 30, 1812. The British were reluctant to respond with martial measures of their own since they were confident that news of the doing away with the Orders in Council would induce America to reverse its decision. Their hopes were dashed with the American demand, and the British refusal, to suspend the practice of impressment. On October 13, His Majesty's Government issued Orders in Council, in effect a declaration of war, authorizing "general reprisals against the ships, goods, and citizens of the United States."

The British government and people were outraged at America's action precipitating war. In their view their struggle with France was not only for national survival, but one championing liberty against French tyranny, which America should be supporting, not

John Calhoun of South Louisiana, one of the Republican "War Hawks" who pushed for war against Britain in 1812.

jeopardizing, by going to war with Britain. John W. Croker, Secretary of the British Admiralty, expressed the sense of sadness and betrayal felt in his country at the actions taken by America. "There are now two free nations," he wrote, "Great Britain and America—let the latter be beware how she raises her parricidal hand against the parent country; her trade and liberty cannot long survive the downfall of British commerce and British freedom. If the citadel [Britain] which now encloses and protects all that remains of European liberty be stormed, what shall defend the American union from the inroads of the despot [Napoleon]?"

In June 1812, President Madison and Congress sounded the call to arms. It remained to be seen how that summons would be answered by the American nation—and responded to by an enemy as powerful as the British.

CHAPTER TWO

Amateurs to Arms

—⟨ೞೞೞ⟩—

IN AUGUST 1812, THOMAS JEFFERSON WROTE TO A FRIEND EXPRESSING THE LONG-standing American belief that Canada could be easily plucked from the British Imperial lion's paw. "The acquisition of Canada this year, as far as the neighborhood of Quebec," he wrote, "will be a mere matter of marching, and will give us experience for the attack on Halifax the next, and the final expulsion of England from the American continent."

Others doubted the notion of a quick occupation of Canada by the United States. *The Yankee*, a Boston newspaper, complained in 1812 that the belief that the British colony would be rapidly overcome by America's might "had taken deep root in Washington . . . and will not be easily exterminated." It went on to question the supposition "that the show of an army, and a few well directed proclamations would unnerve the arm of resistance, and make conquest and reconciliation synonymous." By the time Jefferson penned his August letter, it was already apparent that the United States was not going to succeed in achieving an easy victory in waging what many Americans were calling a "second war for independence." Indeed, the War of 1812 did not turn out to be the romp Jefferson had envisaged.

✦ ✦ ✦

"The moment chosen for the war," wrote James Madison in 1827, "would, therefore, have been well chosen with a reference to the French expedition against Russia; and although not so chosen, the coincidence between the war and the expedition promised at the time to be as it was fortuitous." It is true that Napoleon's invasion of Russia in 1812 was the linchpin for America's war strategy against Britain. In May 1812, 650,000 French and allied soldiers concentrated on Russia's border. The world expected the confrontation to commence that summer and all were convinced that France would be victorious; the Madison administration used the invasion as an opportunity to declare war on the British.

Critics of the administration's military establishment and policies, which they derisively termed "a defense worthy of Republicans," pointed out that the United States was in no condition to fight Great Britain alone. A puny navy could not challenge the Royal Navy, and an army that was small, scattered around the country, under-trained and poorly led, had no chance of waging a successful campaign. But the government in Washington felt confident that the looming Franco-Russian conflict would be just the diversion America needed to aid her in achieving a favorable settlement of her grievances against Britain.

Madison's strategy for a land war called for an American incursion into Canada just as Napoleon's forces marched into Russia. Madison reasoned that after Russia had been subdued by the French, the British would be driven out of Spain and Portugal, and the United Kingdom itself threatened by a Gallic invasion force. As a result, the British would have to keep the bulk of their army and navy at home to ward off the enemy menace, leaving Canada's defenses weak and vulnerable.

At sea, Madison anticipated that the miniscule US Navy would early on be destroyed, captured, or shut-up in American ports by the Royal Navy. He toyed with keeping the few

Napoleon's invasion of Russia in June 1812 was to be the linchpin for America's war strategy against Britain. A French victory, believed the Madison administration, would divert Britain's military resources.

warships the country had in harbor and employing them as floating batteries. However, he changed his tune after being confronted by a number of his senior naval officers. Instead of acting as immobile gun emplacements, the government sanctioned their use as commerce raiders. An additional element of the American naval strategy would be to unleash hundreds of privateers, authorized under letters of marque, to hunt down enemy merchant vessels in an attempt to ruin Britain's seagoing trade, thus pressuring her to come to the peace table.

On the economic front, the United States deployed trade restrictions, collectively known as the restrictive system, composed of embargoes, non-importation and non-intercourse laws. Although this economic coercion system failed in its goal in the years prior to the altercation with Britain, it was revived and put in place during the War of 1812. This is not surprising considering that President Madison had been the chief architect of the restrictive system during the Jefferson administration. The restrictive system proved ineffective, however, since Britain's economy was far less dependent on American commerce than the Republicans imagined, and widespread illegal trading between US citizens and Britain during the war—that is, smuggling—flourished across every American border and coastline.

The United States also waged a diplomatic effort to influence the course of the war. Hoping to prove that all Americans wanted were concessions regarding maritime issues, not war, the Madison administration gave the British hints of its true intentions and desires. Shortly after declaring war, the British Ambassador to the United States, Augustus J. Foster, was sent terms for peace. Critically, the US never clarified its position on Canada during the war, whether it intended to annex the colony or not. However, it seems highly unlikely that once taken, America would ever relinquish all of Canada; the political backlash in the country would have swept the Republicans from office. Furthermore, to promote peace with Britain, Madison wrote to his ambassador in Paris to spread the notion that if the United States and Britain could resolve their differences, "the full tide of indignation with which the [American] public mind here is boiling will be directed against France. War [against France] will be called for by the nation almost *una voce.*" The reason for this paradoxical stance—starting the war, but trying to end it as soon as it began—lay in the fact that American success in the conflict always relied on her ability to successfully carry the fight to the enemy, and in that regard she fell woefully short during the entire conflict.

With a strategy determined, the United States turned to the instruments needed to carry out its implementation: the regular army, the militia, the navy and privateers. Except for the navy, all would prove entirely inadequate for the martial task America had set for itself. The seeds for this condition had been planted years before.

✦ ✦ ✦

Speaking during his 1801 inaugural address, President Thomas Jefferson declared that "a well-disciplined militia, [was] our best reliance in peace, and for the first moments of war, till regulars may relieve them . . ." With these words, the nation's chief executive assured

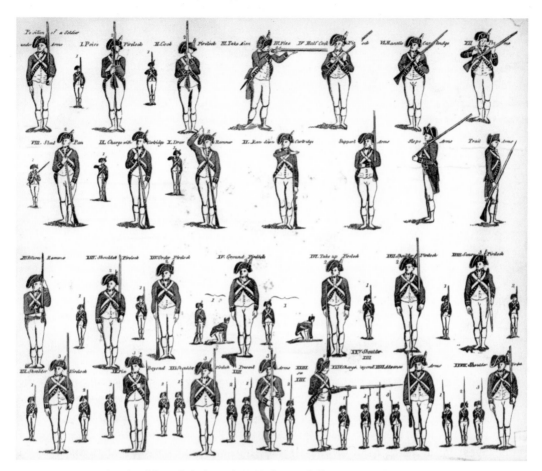

American Manual of Arms of 1802 showing drill exercises for the US Army.

the country that it did not need a standing army and that its safety would be realized by a citizenry trained and organized in arms. When he came to the presidency, the regular United States Army had a strength of 248 officers, 3,794 enlisted men in four infantry and two artillery regiments, two companies of mounted dragoons, and a small engineer corps. By late 1802, Jefferson had reduced the Army's size to a mere 3,040 officers and men in two infantry regiments and one artillery regiment, and an engineer contingent made up of seven officers and ten cadets. Almost a third of the Army's officers had been dismissed! By diminishing its size so drastically, Jefferson intended to prevent a standing army from becoming an instrument of any political party, as the Federalists had attempted to make it. However, under the Republican Party, it was uncertain whether it would be retained as any kind of instrument at all.

The years of Jefferson's administration saw the army little used except for several exploration expeditions and road building projects. Although he objected to a permanent military establishment, Jefferson wanted its officers to be both educated and useful to American society in fields other than just the military art. To that end, he asked Congress to establish in March 1802 the United States Military Academy at West Point, New York, an institution which would serve as the country's first engineering school, and provide the army with intellectual direction and doctrine.

West Point Officer Cadets on parade in early 19th century-style uniforms. Although Jefferson severely reduced the size of the US Army, he did oversee the establishment of the US Military Academy at West Point in 1802.

West Point aside, the Commander-in-Chief was an indifferent administrator for whom the army stood on the margins of his concerns. The result was that pay was low, medical supplies, rations and clothes ran short, resulting in abysmal morale among the officers and men. When the *Leopard-Chesapeake* incident occurred in 1807, the army's strength was below 2,400 men. The national uproar over the *Chesapeake* Affair stirred such anti-British feelings that Jefferson reluctantly secured authorization from Congress in 1808 to raise five new regular regiments of infantry and one each of artillery, riflemen and light dragoons. The aim was to have a force of 10,000 men under arms, but recruitment was so torpid that by 1812 the Army could only muster 6,744 souls.

Compounding the problem of a government that consistently deprived the armed forces of funds and manpower, the United States Army was poorly served by careless leadership. Jefferson's Secretary of War was Henry Dearborn, who eagerly joined with Jefferson in slashing military expenditures during his tenure. Paradoxically, he toyed with certain innovations in the Army, including promoting the use of the Model 1803 Harper's Ferry Rifle and the first US horse artillery. A passionate Republican politician, Dearborn was too close to the administration to shield the army from the cost cutting and indifference that hobbled it so badly under Jefferson.

If Dearborn was so thrift driven, he was at least moderately capable, something that cannot be said of his replacement. When James Madison came to the Presidency in 1809, he named Dr. William Eustis as his Secretary of War. The Cambridge, Massachusetts-born Eustis was a physician who had served during the American Revolutionary War as a

US soldiers in 1813. Left to right: Drummer, US Infantry, wearing British coatee, part of consignment captured by American privateer; Private, US 16th Infantry; Field Officer, 28th US Infantry; (kneeling) Private, 6th US Infantry, wearing summer uniform and the regiment's distinctive bucktail in cap; Private, 17th Infantry, lacking his black coatee. Painting by Ed Dovey.

US soldiers in 1814. Left to right: Fifer, US Infantry, again wearing captured British coatee; Sergeant, 18th Infantry, winter dress including woollen trousers; Lieutenant, 18th Infantry; (seated) Private, 25th Infantry, in famous gray coatee, his haversack painted blue as waterproofing; Private, 7th Infantry. Painting by Ed Dovey.

volunteer surgeon. He lacked meaningful military experience, and like Dearborn before him pursued frugality to extremes. Some of these measures included doing away with the fledging mobile horse artillery company, and his refusal to authorize for cost-cutting reasons the purchase of fruits and vegetables for sick soldiers. He did, however, advocate increasing the size of the army, and the creation of a superintendent of ordnance, a commissary general, and a quartermaster general's department to better supply and move the army. Unfortunately, these sensible reforms, passed by Congress in early 1812, were not in place when hostilities commenced that June. Eustis and his 11 clerks in the department were overwhelmed by their many responsibilities, and his lack of managerial skill only compounded his organization's inability to cope with them. Describing the Secretary's failings, a Pennsylvania Congressman concluded Eustis was "a dead weight in our hands. . . . His unfitness is apparent to everybody but himself."

The process of appointing field grade officers—generals and colonels—was an unmitigated disaster. Madison had to choose between naming Revolutionary War veterans in their 50s and 60s, none of whom had ever reached beyond the rank of colonel, or untrained and untried politicians who had to be unabashed Republicans. The former, according to General Winfield Scott, "had generally, sunk into either sloth, ignorance, or habits of intemperate drinking." Scott went further by describing many of his fellow officers as "swaggers, dependents, decayed gentlemen and others fit for nothing else . . . totally unfit for any military purpose whatever." The political generals chosen by the President were in many instances recommended by Republican Congressmen, who unfortunately, "pressed upon the Executive their own particular friends and dependents." The result was that few of the new officers had any experience of war. One senior general in the United States Army at the start of the conflict was James Wilkinson, financial swindler, confidence man, and traitor to his country, who had the distinction of never having won a battle or lost a court martial. The added irony was that he represented the very officer type the Jeffersonian political establishment so dreaded.

The officers, bad or good, at the start of the war led enlisted men for the most part who were inexperienced in war. Enlistments were for five years, and pay—for privates $5, non-commissioned officers $9, officers up to $20 per month, usually months in arrears—assured that the pool of recruits was always slim. Short-term volunteers were raised but never in sufficient numbers. Only six such regiments were created and the general opinion of their army comrades was that the volunteers were little better than organized bandits who freely engaged in desertion and robbery.

Jefferson's cherished plan to use the militia as the nation's initial and principal defense force never came to fruition. Under the Militia Act of 1792, every free white male between the ages of 18 to 45 was eligible to be in the militia. While each member supplied his own weapon and equipment, the states were to organize them in military formations. Under the law, militiamen were obligated to serve the federal government only three months in any one year. In 1804, all but three states reported that they could raise a total of 525,000 militiamen in time of war. New England and the Western Territories were best prepared.

US Medical Corps Officer (left) and Light Artillery Sergeant on campaign in 1812. Painting by H. Charles McBarron.

The Carolinas could arm half their men, but the other states were lucky if they could supply weapons to one-fifth of their militia. Several states had laws forbidding their militia contingents from leaving the state. Worse, militia officers were state political appointees who put their political expediency above military concerns.

In April 1812, with war coming ever closer, Congress requested the states to field 80,000 militiamen for federal service. The governors of New England refused! Their excuse was that their state's territory was not in danger of foreign invasion and therefore there was no legal reason their militia should be mobilized. Beyond this indifference to serving their country, militias were costly and ill-trained. In writing to President Madison on September 30, 1812, Henry Dearborn, now appointed a general, stated that "The expenses of the Militia are enormous, and they are of little comparative use, except at the commencement of war, and for special emergencies. The sooner we can dispense with their services, the better." During the war, a staggering 450,000 militiamen were at one time or another mustered into United States service, but due to refusal to cross state lines, poor leadership and equipment, only half of this vast number ever saw combat.

Supplying the army was carried out by civilian contractors who were more interested in making a profit than properly filling the needs of the military. The result was that troops went without the basics such as clothes, shoes and other vital equipment for months at a time, and the food they got was usually of poor quality and scant quantity.

In the medical field, doctors attached to the army were few, and in an era of primitive medical science most did not have the skills to combat disease or treat battle wounds properly. Epidemic diseases such as dysentery, typhoid fever, pneumonia, as well as infections, proved fatal to many soldiers during the war. Medicines were always in short supply, and those who survived their wounds or bouts of disease usually did so in spite of their treatment.

The Army had better luck when it came to its small arms, ammunition and cannon. A department to oversee ordnance was in place by 1812 and ran smoothly during the war. With established federal armories at Springfield, Massachusetts and Harpers Ferry, Virginia, and with additional factories built after 1812, the manufacture and repair of muskets and rifles and production of ammunition was unimpeded. Cannon were purchased from private foundries, such as the one operated in Connecticut by Eli Whitney.

✦ ✦ ✦

In contrast to the Army, the US Navy entered the War of 1812 with a surprisingly high degree of professionalism and technological superiority. The country's youngest military service was authorized by an Act of Congress in March 1794, in response to attacks on American merchant vessels by North African pirates during the Barbary Wars. It had expanded between 1798 and 1805, but no new frigates had been launched since 1800. Saddled with the parsimonious and pacifist Jefferson administration, the blue water navy had to fight for every dollar of appropriations from a government which spent much of its limited budget on gunboats for harbor defense, not on an ocean-going fighting force. As a result, American naval strength was small, and hampered by a lack of navy yards that could adequately maintain the ships. Consequently, expectations for the effectiveness, and even the survivability of the tiny United States Navy were extremely low at the start of the War of 1812, but they would prove their doubters wrong.

In January 1812, the US Navy had only 14 commissioned warships: three 44-gun frigates, three smaller armed frigates sporting 28 to 38 guns, two 18-gun sloops, six brigs with 12 to 16 cannon each, with two more refitted frigates mounting 38 guns added to that number during the year. Opposing these were over 500 active duty combat vessels of the British Royal Navy. But unlike the Army, the American Navy was stiffened by about 500 career officers, many of whom had seen combat against the French in the Quasi-War of 1798–1800 and the Barbary Pirates of North Africa. Most were young men in their 30s and 40s, like David Porter Jr. and John Rogers, whose bombast and egotism reflected their high level of confidence and fighting spirit. Others such as William Bainbridge, "had all of [Stephen] Decatur's pride and vanity and touchy sense of honor with none of his dash," were nonetheless formidable naval fighters. Stephen Decatur was the hero of the Barbary Wars with a string of naval victories to his name.

With all this combat service, there was no dearth of skilled and experienced sailors. The Navy listed 5,230 on its rolls, 2,346 of them fighting crews, the rest stationed in dockyards, coast defenses, and the Great Lakes. The term of service was for one year and pay ranged from $6 to $18 a month depending on job skills. As part of the Navy, a 1,000-man Marine Corps was authorized, but it never reached a strength of more than 500 during the war. Its members served as port and ship security and as naval landing parties.

Despite the severe size differential between the US and British navies, the Americans had some distinct advantages that counted strongly in combat. American ship crews were larger than their British counterparts, and American frigate design made for faster craft with greater maneuverability to buttress the considerable punch of their superior 24-pounder guns.

Despite the anticipation of war with Britain, Congress and the President made no effort to expand their fleet, even though the Navy Department warned that it would require 12 ships-of-the-line, each carrying 74 cannon, and 20 frigates to adequately safeguard the American coastline. Initial victories in 1812 spurred the administration to initiate a new naval building program intended to construct six 44-gun frigates and four 74-gun ships-of-the-line, but none of these were either completed or saw service during the war.

Besides the operations of the Navy, the United States resorted to privateering with great success. Most privateers were merchant traders, the largest contingent coming from Massachusetts, with some 150 vessels acting under letters of marque; that is, commissions to commit hostile acts against enemy shipping. Their reward for this blend of patriotism and profit was the money they made from the capture of enemy goods and ships. About 526 ships of all types and sizes, usually armed with one or two long guns, and able to race across coastal waters, were loosed upon British shipping. The best ship model used for this venture was the two-masted Baltimore clipper schooner. America's privateers, raiding

USS Constellation *clashes with French* L'Insurgente *in February 1799 during the Quasi War of 1798–1800. Such undeclared warfare against the French Republic meant that American seamen were far more combat experienced than their army compatriots. Painting by John W. Schmidt.*

the seas of North and South America and Europe, proved to be the most effective weapons aimed at British trade during the war.

✦ ✦ ✦

"For this government," wrote Lord Liverpool, Britain's Prime Minister in June 1812, "the American War, in truth, is little more than an annoying distraction, albeit at a time we can ill afford it." Engaged in a fight for its very existence against Revolutionary France and the Emperor Napoleon, British national attention had been exclusively focused on that struggle since 1793, while maintaining its economic influence around the world.

Of primary concern in North America were its several colonies north of the United States border: Lower Canada (modern Quebec); Upper Canada (present day Ontario); Nova Scotia; New Brunswick; Newfoundland; Prince Edward Island; and Cape Breton Island. Making up today's nation of Canada, these British colonies by the early 19th century had developed a thriving economy based on the fur trade, fisheries, wheat farming and lumber. The last was of vital interest to Britain, since as European-sourced ship building timber and masts became restricted, Canadian sources of this raw material made up the shortfall. Here was a vast supply of wood needed by the Royal Navy and the world's largest merchant fleet to keep it afloat; the defense of this important strategic supply was perhaps the most powerful motivating factor for keeping Canadian colonies in British hands.

The question for the United Kingdom in 1812 was how best to preserve these holdings against the young Republic to the south. In October 22, 1811, official instructions to Sir George Prevost, Governor-in-Chief and supreme military commander in British North America, were very specific. In case of war with the United States, British forces in Canada were not to commence offense operations, "except for the purpose of preventing or repelling Hostilities or unavoidable Emergencies." Thus, the initial British strategy for the protection of Canada from American attack was set. It was a realistic decision based on the fact that the war against Napoleon was straining British imperial resources to the limit.

With the population of the USA at seven and a half million, versus only about 500,000 British subjects living in Canada, the manpower odds against the latter were crushing. Only about 7,000 troops were stationed in the area in 1812, a vast region stretching 1,300 miles from the Atlantic Ocean to Lake Michigan. Nor could additional soldiers be easily found. The bulk of the British Army under the Duke of Wellington was tied up in the Iberian Peninsula fighting the French. Since January 1812, he had been successfully driving the enemy from large parts of Spain. To take troops away from him at this critical juncture would have weakened his momentum and given the French an opportunity to recover. Furthermore, the transfer of men and material from Spain to Canada—a distance of over 3,000 watery miles—would have taken months, by which time Canada might have already fallen to the Americans.

Stephen Decatur boards a Barbary Pirate gunboat in 1804. Decatur's heroic victories were an inspiration to American naval commanders in the War of 1812. Painting by Dennis M Carter.

Another salient reason for the British to remain on the defensive was the attitude of many of its inhabitants—the fiercely independent French-speaking Canadians, and the Americans residing in the provinces. Some of the 80,000 residents of Upper Canada were Loyalist refugees from the American Revolution who had no sympathy for the United States, but there were many more westward moving Americans who either had little interest in the coming conflict or were actively pro-American. Lower Canada contained the largest centers of population, such as Montreal and Quebec. The settlers of this region were overwhelmingly French, and their loyalty as the conflict approached was uncertain. Overall, Canadian demographics demanded a defensive stance, at least at the war's beginning.

On the high seas, the British plan was to sweep American war vessels from the ocean, but the European war kept much of the Royal Navy confined to a role of blockading French ports, greatly reducing the number of British ships available to tackle the American Navy and its privateers. Control of the Great Lakes was another objective of the Royal Navy. Denying their use to the enemy would be a key part of its overall defensive strategy, which would greatly impede any American incursion into Canada, and then, when an offensive was finally assumed, serve as a watery highway into American territory. Along the US coast, British naval strategy, hand-in-hand with its objective of destroying American commerce, envisioned creating a "wooden wall" of ships in order to blockade enemy warships and privateers in port. In the process, it hoped to strangle American seaborne trade by preventing cargo from entering or leaving the United States.

✦   ✦   ✦

"There, it all depends upon that article whether we do the business or not." Thus declared the Duke of Wellington on the eve of the battle of Waterloo—"that article" being the British regular infantryman. At the start of 1812, there were only 5,600 British regulars serving in Canada. These troops would remain the backbone of the defense of British North America for the entire war. They would give outstanding service during the conflict due to their training, esprit, and familiarity with the country and peoples of the area. While a small reinforcement of regulars trickled into the theater in 1813, it would not be until the close of the European war against France that tens of thousands more British soldiers, mostly from Wellington's army, were sent to North America.

Among the British regular units found in Canada at the start of hostilities were the 8th (King's) Regiment, the 41st, 49th (both having been in Canada for a decade and a half), the 98th, 99th, 100th Regiments of Foot, the 10th Royal Veteran Battalion, and 450 gunners of the Royal Artillery Regiment. Also counted in the ranks as regulars were the 104th Regiment of Foot (New Brunswick Fencibles), the Royal Newfoundland Regiment of Fencible Infantry, the Canadian Fencibles, and the Nova Scotia Fencibles. These Fencible formations were Canadian-raised colonial regular units within the British Army establishment, trained on the British model, and led by British officers. Another fine fighting force raised in Canada, this one from among Scottish settlers, was the Glengarry Light Infantry Regiment, which saw much action in Upper Canada during the war.

Lower Canada raised 6,500 men for military duty in early 1812. Their members were in the majority French Canadians who, as one British officer put it, "perhaps did not love the English Government or people, but they loved the Americans less." The Canadian Voltigeurs was one of the area's units mustered in and was listed as one of the British regular forces on the Army Returns.

Regular soldiers in British service were traditionally recruited from the laboring class. Pay ranged from one shilling a day for a private, to a shilling and 2-1/4 pennies for an infantry corporal, and a shilling and 6-3/4 pennies for a sergeant. Deductions for lodgings while on the march and other "necessaries" soon reduced the soldier's wages to a pittance. What made them so formidable in combat, especially compared to their American counterparts, was the intensity of their training, iron discipline, and being well equipped and led.

The line officers commanding British soldiers were recruited from the privileged class and could obtain higher rank, at an official rate of purchase, up to the grade of Lieutenant- Colonel. Most British officers, from ensigns to army generals, were not professionally trained in the arts of war, but coming from a sporting class, they instinctively provided the inspiration and leadership required to command men in battle. Furthermore, war, like sporting events, included competition, and success in war meant promotion, honor and glory. Those officers who served in colonial stations, like Canada, were usually not financially able to buy their way into a prestigious regiment serving in England or Spain. As a result, many of these men were keen on making the Army their vocation and excelling at it. The result was a high proportion of good combat leaders facing the Americans in the War of 1812.

Fortunately for Great Britain, the senior officers in command of the army in Canada at the start of the War of 1812 were up to the task of defending their charge. They were professional soldiers capable of organizing, training and leading troops in battle, as well as competent to deal with the problems of civil administration. They ranged from the cautious Lieutenant-General Sir George Prevost to the extremely audacious Major-General Isaac Brock, the prudent Major-General Roger Sheaffe, the detached Major-General Baron Francis de Rottenburg, and the persistent Lieutenant-General Gordon Drummond. They also had the singular advantage of facing American generals in 1812 who were poor military leaders due to inexperience, and in some cases pure incompetence.

Besides the British Army Regulars and trained colonial units, Canada possessed a considerable militia force, at least on paper: 11,000 men from Upper Canada; 54,000 from Lower Canada—termed Lower Canadian Sedentary Militia; 12,000 from Nova Scotia; the New Brunswick militia 4,500 men strong; and small contingents from the other Atlantic provinces of Newfoundland, Prince Edward and the Cape Breton Islands. According to General Prevost, the militia, especially from Lower Canada, was "a mere posse, ill armed and without discipline." Regardless of Prevost's opinion, these French-Canadians were a sturdy lot, good hunters, excellent marksmen, and adept at Indian-style skirmishing in the vast Canadian forests. At the commencement of the war, most of the militia did not possess uniforms but wore homespun clothes. Five battalions of Lower Canadian militia were raised in 1812 and did good service during the conflict. The Upper Canadian militia provided eight battalions of 4,000 men prior to the war, a number largely filled by revenge-seeking Loyalist refugees from the United States.

Like that of the United States, Canadian militia forces were present in virtually every major engagement of the war. Besides their combat role, they served as garrison troops as well as providing labor for the construction of and the repair of fortifications, and the transport of supplies.. While surprised at the reliability of the militia during the war, British authorities still had to contend with their high desertion rate, a problem never satisfactorily solved during the conflict.

One other force available to help the British fight for Canada was the Indians. After their defeat by William Henry Harrison at the battle of Tippecanoe, on November 6, 1811, the Shawnee leader Tecumseh led his people to join the British at Amherstburg, also known as Fort Malden, on the northwest shore of Lake Erie. There, he and his people came under the authority of the Indian Department, which was charged with carrying on diplomatic and military relations with all Indian tribes in British North America. Its staff of 100 lieutenants, captains and interpreters was responsible for securing military cooperation

Lord Liverpool, British Prime Minister during the War of 1812. Based on portrait by Thomas Lawrence.

between the Indians in Upper and Lower Canada and the military by providing instructors and support for the Native American contingents fighting with the British. Tecumseh's 600 warriors were a welcome addition to the British defense of Upper Canada in 1812, and proved their worth before the year was out.

Of vital aid to any defense of Canada was the Royal Navy. But when America declared war on Britain, its naval power was fully committed to the struggle against Napoleon. In September 1812, three months after America and Britain went to war, the Royal Navy had no more than 79 warships in the western hemisphere. These included 11 ships-of-the-line, 34 frigates, and about the same number of smaller schooners, sloops and brigs. Moreover, this paltry force was spread thinly, escorting merchant shipping, protecting the Saint Lawrence River, chasing American war vessels, and hunting enemy privateers. Thus, the British Admiralty could not effectively in the first six months of the war blockade the America coastline in order to render United States naval forces impotent, or cut American trade.

The Royal Navy had 1,000 warships in its arsenal with over 550 operational at any one time. Consuming a quarter of Britain's annual budget, the Navy was the most professional and well-trained maritime force in the world. In 1812, its fleets were manned by over

British Army Ensign and Colour Sergeant. Print published in 1813.

113,600 sailors, but the insatiable need for more seamen never abated. Yet the largest navy in the world did have its weaknesses.

Desertion from ships by their crew was endemic, and no amount of impressment or flogging ever solved the problem. The result was that even with higher wages being paid to common seamen after the naval mutinies of the 1790s, the Navy had to habitually man its fleets with smaller than required complements.

After its victory at the battle of Trafalgar in 1805, the Royal Navy concentrated on economic warfare against France by blockading the French coast. Such a task required a large number of vessels, and after 1805 these were mass-produced, based on a smaller ship design, with less armament and crew than the newer and technically more advanced American frigates. The result was an imbalance in combat capability when, early in the war, one-on-one battles occurred between American and British warships.

If British ship designs were not the best to fight the Americans in 1812, and the dearth of crewmen was an impediment to the proper performance of a ship, there was little to complain about when it came to officers of the Royal Navy. They came from all classes of British society: the aristocracy, the professions, business and commerce, navy families and merchant traders. There was no purchase of rank in the navy—six years at sea and passing a seamanship examination was the qualification demanded before receiving an officer's commission. Merit and practical experience was the key to the Royal Navy's leadership excellence and dominance of the world's oceans.

In tandem with the activities of the blue water navy, British occupation of the Great Lakes was vital to the defense of Canada in 1812. Under the command of the Provincial Marine, the small colonial-operated squadrons that plied Lake Ontario, Lake Erie and Huron were instrumental in interdicting American troop and supply movements across those waterways. It was a portent of things to come—to invade or defend Canada, the Lakes had to be secured.

✦   ✦   ✦

On July 12, 1812, an American military force crossed the Detroit River, north of Lake Erie, and entered upon Canadian soil. Taking control of the village of Sandwich, this incursion was the opening shot in the War of 1812—a war for which America was unprepared and wanted a quick conclusion, and one in which the British were very uncertain of success. Canada was now in abeyance, and only time would tell if its defense forces could fend off the attackers.

CHAPTER THREE

Disaster at Detroit,
Debacle at Queenston

AN OFFICIAL ORDER, DATED JUNE 24, 1812 ARRIVED AT THE SMALL TOWN OF
Detroit on July 9, from Secretary of War William Eustis. Addressed to Brigadier-General
William Hull, commander of the American military forces on the northwestern frontier,
it suggested that if Hull considered his force "equal to the enterprise, consistent with the
safety of your own posts," Hull was to capture British-held Fort Malden, which lay across
the river from Detroit, and "extend your conquests as circumstances may justify." The
message went on to warn the general he could not expect cooperation from the American
forces further east under Major-General Henry Dearborn, since the latter did not yet have
an "adequate force" to commence his own operations. This part of the communication
was especially worrisome since Dearborn's task was to fix the British in place along the
Niagara Front so they could not move to interfere with Hull's advance.

William Hull and his army found themselves at Detroit in 1812 as a result of the
Madison administration's plan for that year's military campaign against Canada. The strategy
envisioned four thrusts north of the US-Canadian border. The main advance was to start
from Lake Champlain and aim for Montreal. Subsidiary forces were to move from Sackets
Harbor (originally spelled Sackett's), located on the western fringe of Lake Ontario, to
Kingston on the north bank of the St. Lawrence River as its target; and from western New
York State, a strike across the Niagara River was to be made. Hull's march against Fort
Malden in western Upper Canada, just across the Detroit River from the town of the same
name, completed the quartet of martial gambits. Details for the movement, including the

Heavily wooded Canadian frontier land in the early 19th century.

timing and coordination of the various American columns, were not worked out ahead of the declaration of war, and cooperation between the widely separated forces was not expected.

The United States government had concerns about the vulnerability of the vast expanse of land known as the Old Northwest Territory, which at the time was being sub-jected to continuing and destructive Indian depredations under the skillful hand of Tecum-seh. Its 300-mile-long border stretched from Fort Mackinac east to Detroit, and was thinly guarded by only 420 United States Regulars in seven widely scattered stockade forts—the principal one at Detroit with its 120-man garrison, the others housing an average of 50 to 60 men each. Illinois, Indiana and Michigan were so sparsely populated (less than 5,000 American citizens) that there were few militia available to back up the Federal troops in the territory. The US government reasoned that should war break out between the United States and Great Britain, many of the Great Lakes Indian tribes would join the British, threatening further America's hold on the area. The nation's western flank, especially around Detroit, had to be protected. Secretary of War Eustis was certain that the presence of an American army would accomplish this by subduing the Indians and providing force for an invasion of Upper Canada. To those ends, he started to assemble such an army early in 1812. Prior to war with Britain, American military strategy was being dictated by Indian raids in the Old Northwest Territory.

Thus, 59-year-old William Hull found himself in the first week of July at the important border town of Detroit, whose 800 residents—mainly French-Canadians—were as raw and ill-disciplined as most of the small American force he brought with him. Hull seemed the logical choice for command in that region. Born in Derby, Connecticut on June 24, 1753, he pursued a legal career after graduating from Yale University in 1772. During the American Revolution he performed well at the battles of White Plains, Trenton, Princeton, Saratoga and Monmouth Court House, rising to the rank of Major in 1777. Two years later, he won promotion to Lieutenant-Colonel after he spearheaded General "Mad" Anthony Wayne's nighttime bayonet assault against British-held Stoney Point in New York.

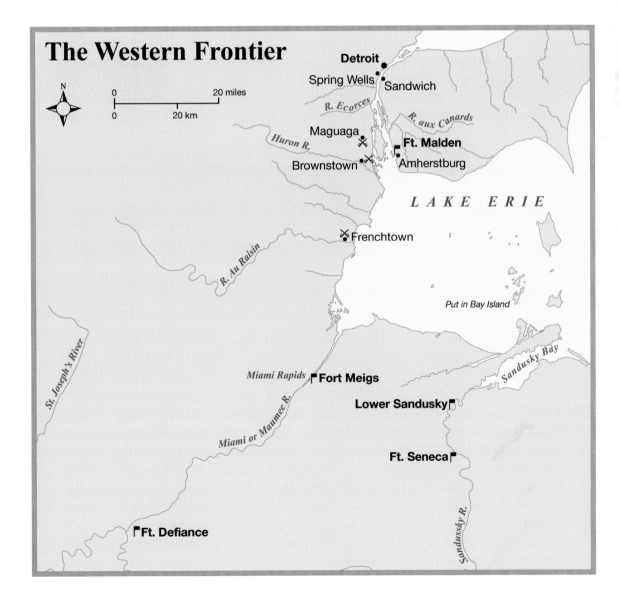

He served as assistant Inspector General under Baron von Steuben before he was made full Colonel and then assigned command of the American defenses at West Point, New York. After the war, Hull took up the practice of law in Massachusetts and served as a Major-General in that state's militia. During the 1788 Shay's Rebellion, he was part of General Benjamin Lincoln's army that crushed the uprising. He became a Republican and was elected an Old Bay State Senator and judge before being named by President Thomas Jefferson the first Governor of the Michigan Territory in 1805, a position he held at the commencement of the War of 1812.

While in Washington, DC in February 1812, to plead with the government for more resources to shield the Northwest Territory from Indian attacks, Hull was offered command of the forces then gathering for the Detroit frontier. Hull refused on the grounds that he did not wish to relinquish his post as governor of the territory. Nevertheless, Hull was again approached with the offer of leading the undertaking. This time he reluctantly accepted and on April 8 the US Senate confirmed his appointment as a Brigadier-General in the United States Army and commander of the expeditionary force gathering in the northwest. Meanwhile, troops were being gathered for that venture.

In March, Eustis had written Ohio Governor Return Meigs to muster 1,200 militiamen for the Detroit expedition. The required number of men, mostly volunteers, were assembled at Dayton, Ohio by April 29 and formed into three regiments. Colonel Duncan McArthur, Colonel James Findlay, and Colonel Lewis Cass, Ohio politicians all, were elected to command the 1st, 2nd, and 3rd Ohio Militia Infantry Regiments, respectively. None had any real experience in military matters. In addition, Lieutenant-Colonel James Miller, in charge of the United States 4th Infantry Regiment, 300-men-strong and stationed at Vincennes, Indiana, was ordered to move his unit to Dayton to join the expedition headed for Detroit.

Before Hull set out to join his new command, titled the Army of the Northwest, he urged President Madison to create a naval force on Lake Erie to ensure American control of that body of water. He recommended a force of at least 3,000 men be sent to Detroit, and that enough supplies be forwarded there to sustain an advance into Canada, or if need arose, defense of the town before navigation on Lake Erie was closed, as was likely, by the enemy. None of Hull's suggestions were implemented.

+   +   +

On June 1, Hull started the army on its march to Urbana, Ohio, on the border with Indian country. After arriving at Urbana on the 7th, a peace council between the Americans and Wyandotte, Shawnee and Mingo chiefs concluded a treaty that allowed the Americans to cross the Indian lands and build a road and fortifications to protect it. The Indians also pledged their neutrality. On the 15th, the army left Urbana, constructing its own road and bridges for 75 miles through the swampy wilderness. Four blockhouses were built along the route to protect the road and important river crossings. The army marched through the wooded country in typical military fashion: in two columns, with the supply, baggage and artillery trains between them, a strong front and rear guard, and flanked by riflemen and cavalry.

Hull and his men crossed the rapids of the Maumee River (which entered Lake Erie at its southwestern tip), near modern Toledo on June 30. He chartered the schooner *Cuyahoga* to transport the army's heavy baggage, medical supplies and the sick, as well as his military papers to Detroit. Unfortunately, the *Cuyahoga*, sailing close to Fort Malden, was captured, and with it a record of the American army's strength and plans. The British now had a clear idea of the size and strength of their opposition as well as its mission.

American border town of Detroit in 1800 was guarded by a British-built Revolutionary War era fort.

Meanwhile, Hull reached Detroit on July 5 with 2,050 men. These included the Ohio volunteers and militia (1,592 men), minus the garrisons of the four blockhouses guarding the line-of-communications back to Ohio, and the sick captured with the *Cuyahoga*, leaving a balance of 1,450 Ohio men; the US 4th Infantry with 264 soldiers; 135 regulars of the US 1st Infantry Regiment; and 200 of the 1st Michigan Militia.

Detroit was guarded by a British-built Revolutionary War era bastion known as Fort Detroit, situated on high ground behind the town, which blocked the fort's command of the river. The post encompassed three acres, was formed in a quadrilateral shape, each side extending 100 yards, had a parapet 11 feet high and 12 feet thick, with a six-foot-deep and 12-foot-wide ditch studded with 12-foot-high cedar staves at the bottom. Thirty-four pieces of artillery, ranging from 3 to 24-pounders were mounted for action. Some of the installation's armament might have been intended for use on the only American warship on Lake Erie—the 14-gun brig *Adams,* which unfortunately for the Americans was being rebuilt at Detroit and would not be available for service in the coming campaign.

Across the Detroit River (actually a 27-mile-long strait between Lake Erie and Lake St. Clair), and a mile downstream from Detroit, stood the Canadian village of Sandwich (modern day Windsor), which the Americans occupied on July 12; 15 miles south of Windsor was the larger town of Amherstburg. Both population centers, and the border area around them, were guarded by Fort Malden, a quadrilateral fortification with four bastions and an advanced redoubt, an escarpment surrounding the whole, armed with 20 cannon, built in 1796.

The British commander of the Western District of Upper Canada was Lieutenant-Colonel Thomas Bligh St. George, whose ground troops included 300 men of the 41st Regiment of Foot, 850 Canadian militiamen, a detachment of the Royal Artillery Regiment, and 400 Indians. Of equal importance was the naval contingent at St. George's disposal: the brig *Queen Charlotte*, mounting 16 cannon, the schooner *General Hunter* with six guns,

The British captured Fort Dearborn on August 15, 1812, and their Shawnee Indian allies massacred the American prisoners. This contemporary illustration of the scene captures the revulsion felt by the Americans at Indian assaults, which would include torture and scalping.

and *Lady Prevost* with ten. These vessels, as well as a number of merchant ships, gave undisputed control of the waters around Detroit to the British.

Faced with entering enemy territory, Hull began to have doubts about his chances of success. "The British command the water, and the Savages," Hull wrote to Secretary Eustis on July 9. "I do not think the force here equal to the reduction of Amherstburg. You therefore must not be too sanguine." Part of Hull's concern was the lack of enough boats to ferry his men over the river, only sufficient to transport 400 men at a time. Nevertheless, after sending one of his regiments on July 11th south of Detroit to feint a crossing there, the army passed over the waterway to the north of the town the next day. The weak British forces screening the river withdrew to Fort Malden. The American triumph was marred only by the refusal of 100 Ohio militiamen to tread on Canadian soil.

Upon arrival on the eastern shore, Hull erected a fortified camp and sited artillery batteries on both sides of the Detroit River to deny British warships entry to the upper lakes. He then issued a proclamation to the Canadians promising a policy of conciliation on the part of the United States. He dispatched foraging and reconnaissance parties to gather food and intelligence from the area. One of the reconnoitering groups, under Colonel Cass, scouted toward the Canard River bridge, about 12 miles south of Sandwich on July 16. Although ordered by Hull not to cross the Canard River, or engage the enemy, Cass disobeyed his superior's injunction when he saw that the bridge, which spanned the 30-yard-wide river, was intact, and guarded by only 50 British soldiers. Leaving a small party of men concealed at the north end of the bridge, Cass took the balance of the 280 Americans with him and forded the Canard five miles below the bridge. Upon reaching the bridge from the south, they were met by determined British, Canadian and Indian musket fire. After a firefight that saw the Americans pushed back three times, the now reinforced British were forced to withdraw from Cass's front as the American squad north of the river stormed and cleared the bridge.

With the capture of the bridge over the Canard River, the only natural obstacle between the Americans and Fort Malden had been removed. But instead of holding the bridge for the passage of the army and a march on Malden, Hull dithered, expressing fears that Cass was too far from the American position at Sandwich, and that the British would land from the Detroit River above the bridge and cut off any force stationed there. Without support from the army commander, Cass was forced to give up his prize and returned to the main American camp.

✦ ✦ ✦

Hull remained inactive at Sandwich and reported to Eustis that only by way of a regular siege and heavy artillery bombardment could he take Fort Malden. Meantime, mass defections of the Canadian militia and Indians were taking place on the British side. Hearing of this, the American commander felt that time was with him, especially with the attitude of the Indian tribes favoring neutrality, but that all changed with the alarming news of the fall of Fort Mackinac.

Fort Mackinac, situated on an island in the strait between Lakes Michigan and Huron in the heart of Indian country, was garrisoned by 61 US troops and a few nine-pounder cannon under Lieutenant Porter Hanks. Understanding that its capture would have great effect on the Indians of the Northwest, Major-General Isaac Brock, both British military commander and provincial governor of Upper Canada, ordered the fort's capture. The British officer tasked with this assignment by Brock was Captain Charles Roberts, post commandant of Fort St. Joseph, located 45 miles north of the Americans at Fort Mackinac. After assembling 625 men, including regulars, Indians and Canadians, and two six-pounder cannon, Roberts sailed for the American position on the schooner *Caledonia* on July 16. Next day, after dragging one of his artillery pieces to a hill which commanded the American fort, Roberts demanded the surrender of the post. Hanks, who had only just learned that war had been declared, surrendered without a shot being fired.

The impact of the fall of Fort Mackinac was swift as it was dramatic. The Indian tribes, which had been cowed by Hull's presence on Canadian soil, were now certain that the British would throw the Americans out of Canada. As a result, they immediately flocked to the British camp, providing the manpower advantage that would determine the course of the 1812 campaign in western Upper Canada. Another effect of the fall of Mackinac was the abandonment of Fort Dearborn, in Illinois Territory, and the massacre on August 15 by Indians of 52 American soldiers, militia and civilians ordered to leave there by Hull earlier that summer. The killings there elevated the American fear of the Indians in the region even more.

Learning of the fall of Fort Mackinac on July 28, Hull pleaded for reinforcements from the governors of Ohio and Kentucky to the tune of 2,000 men. While continuing preparations for the siege of Fort Malden, he urgently requested a diversion on the Niagara front to assist him. He needed all the help he could get because a string of events was about to threaten any chance of his success.

First, Hull needed fresh supplies which could only reach him—thanks to British control of Lake Erie—by moving the 200 miles from Urbana overland through the same Indian territory the Americans had marched through on their way to Detroit in June. The supply problem was seriously compounded by the fall of Fort Mackinac, as the Wyandotte Indians—the tribe through whose land Hull's line-of-supply ran back to Ohio—defected to the Redcoats. To safeguard the convoy he was expecting, Hull assigned Major Thomas Van Horne, and 200 men to meet it at River Raisin, south of Detroit. Near Brownstown, on August 5, the Americans were ambushed by about two dozen Indians led by Tecumseh. After a few musket volleys from the Indians hidden in the forest, the Americans took flight, losing 17 killed, 12 wounded and two captured, in what became known as the battle of Brownstown. The Indians suffered one killed and another wounded. As a result, the supply convoy led by Captain Henry Brush remained blocked and could not reach Detroit.

Determined to take Fort Malden, Hull went ahead with his plan of attack until he received word that the British had received reinforcements of regular troops from their forces on the Niagara. This abruptly changed his mind about moving against Malden, and he decided to retreat across the river to Detroit. Under the circumstances it would have been better for the Americans to have withdrawn to River Raisin; by doing so, they would have considerably shortened their supply lines. As it was, Hull's position was becoming more precarious each day as a growing number of Indians went over to the British and their combined forces started moving east from the Fort Mackinac region towards Detroit.

After crossing to the American side of the Detroit River, Hull sent Colonel Miller and 600 men to the Rouge River to open communications to the south and meet up with Brush's urgently needed supply column. Shadowing the Americans was a 400-man force of British regulars, Canadian militia and Tecumseh-led Indians, all under the command of Captain Adam Muir, 41st Regiment of Foot. This detachment had been sent out by the new commander of the western Upper Canadian frontier region, Lieutenant-Colonel Henry Proctor, who had superseded St. George. Adam set up an ambush on August 9th at the Indian village of Maguaga, with the British and Canadians on the right, and the Indians in the woods to the left.

The battle of Maguaga started at 4:00pm, when the advance guard of the American force was fired on by the concealed enemy. The Americans held their ground, allowing the rest of the corps to form a line of battle. After half an hour, a party of Indians was driven back onto the British lines by a bayonet charge ordered by Miller. The retreating Indians were then mistakenly fired on by the British. The Indians, in their turn, fired at their allies thinking they were the enemy. This friendly fire caused the Redcoats to fall back. Muir, who had been twice wounded, was able to halt the retreat and reform his lines. But the Indians had withdrawn and were being hotly pursued by the Americans off to Muir's left. Hearing the Americans moving in that direction, the British officer thought he was being flanked, and fearing being cut off from the river, he took to his boats and returned to Malden. The Americans lost 18 killed and 64 wounded, while British losses were five killed, 15 wounded, and two captured.

The American success at Maguaga should have resulted in Miller proceeding to meet the needed supply convoy and the 200 reinforcements under Brush still at River Raisin, but the colonel and his severely mauled detachment remained inactive until ordered to return to Detroit on the 19th. A significant opportunity to improve Hull's military situation had been lost. The attempt to remedy it was not made until August 14 when Hill ordered out Colonels McArthur and Cass with 350 men to try to reach Brush and his supply train near the Huron River and bring them to Detroit.

As Hull hunkered down in Detroit, Colonel Lewis Cass wrote to a friend about the inadequacies of his commander and how "Our situation is become critical." Meanwhile, the British commander Brock assembled forces at Long Point, the chief British staging area on Lake Erie, in order to channel reinforcements to the Detroit front. He sent 300 regulars and militia from there to Malden and organized his small army into three "brigades" of 250 men each to be led by Proctor in an offensive to drive the Americans out of Canada. On August 15, Brock moved his force north across the Canard River bridge. Meanwhile, Proctor had installed a gun battery of one 18-pounder, two 12-pounders, and two 5.5-inch howitzers at Sandwich with which to bombard Detroit.

Upon arrival at Sandwich on the 15th, Brock wrote to Hull demanding his surrender, threatening "that the numerous Indians who have attached themselves to my troops, will be beyond my control the moment the contest commences." Although Hull rejected the ultimatum, his concern for the safety of the American non-combatants in Detroit— among them his daughter and her two children—lay heavily on his mind.

The British opened up that same day with their artillery located at Sandwich. In addition, the guns of the *Queen Charlotte* and *General Hunter* went into action. Both sides exchanged fire for a good part of the day while Brock prepared to move his men west of the river. That evening, Tecumseh and 600 braves, supervised by Lieutenant Colonel Elliott of the Indian Department, crossed over to the Detroit side of the river. As shells rained down on Detroit town and its fort, McArthur and Cass vainly sought Brush at the Huron River, but the latter had not moved from River Raisin to meet them. The two militia officers, low on food, marched back to within three miles of Detroit without notifying Hull of their return or close proximity.

Daylight on the 16th saw the artillery duel start again, while the British and Canadian infantry crossed the river at Spring Wells without opposition. At first Brock took up a strong position hoping to lure the Americans into attacking him, but once he discovered that the detachment under McArthur and Cass were not at Detroit, he moved on the town immediately with his 330 regulars, 400 militia, and three 6-pounder cannon. As they arrived near Fort Detroit, the post's artillery, although manned and ready to deliver fire, remained silent. The reason—the Americans were about to surrender.

As Brock neared the fort, Hull learned that Tecumseh's warriors had entered the town and the Michigan militia had deserted their posts. Furthermore, the whereabouts of McArthur and Cass's men were not known, the British artillery barrage was becoming increasingly effective, and Hull succumbed to his anxiety over the safety of the women and children under his care. He feared an Indian massacre. He sent his son to Brock with an offer of surrender. The surrender terms included not only the troops in Fort Detroit, but also McArthur and Cass's men, and Brush's detachment on River Raisin. Under the terms agreed, the American militiamen and volunteers were paroled and sent back to the United States, while the US regulars were transported to Montreal to await exchange. Only Brush refused to lay down his arms and instead took his men back to Ohio.

Two years later, in 1814, Hull got the court martial he had been demanding since his release from British captivity on parole in late 1812. After dismissing the charge of treason, the Military Court did find him guilty of cowardice and neglect of duty and ordered him to be drummed out of the US Army and shot. President Madison approved the sentence but commuted the penalty. Politics demanded someone be blamed for the disaster in the west, and William Hull was the convenient scapegoat. Hull spent the rest of his life in a futile effort to exonerate himself. He died on November 29, 1825, the embodiment of ineptitude in a poorly fought campaign.

The capitulation of the American army at Detroit pushed the United States almost

American commander William Hull surrenders Detroit to the British Major-General Isaac Brock on August 16, 1812.

entirely out of the Old Northwest Territory, encouraged the Indians in the region to join with the British en masse, and sheared off one of the prongs of the American invasion of Canada. It was the beginning of a number of military setbacks for the country in a war that had barely begun.

✦ ✦ ✦

While the spring and summer of 1812 passed, and William Hull's northwest campaign unfolded, no military action took place in the east of the USA. That entire period was spent in preparation, but not pushed with urgency. In April, militia forces were ordered to Niagara, Oswego and Sackets Harbor to garrison those points on the northern border with Canada, but no other military activity was initiated by the US government for the protection of that frontier or for the build-up of forces for a strike into Canada. The man responsible for this American inaction was Henry Dearborn. ⌄

Dearborn was born in North Hampton, New Hampshire, on February 23, 1751. A doctor before the Revolutionary War, he joined the state militia and fought at Bunker Hill and in Benedict Arnold's Canadian expedition, where he was captured at Quebec. He fought also at Saratoga, Monmouth Court House, and in the 1779 campaign against the Iroquois, ending the war as Assistant Quartermaster on the staff of George Washington. After the war he held public offices in Maine, and was a Major-General of militia. As a reliable Republican, he was named President Jefferson's Secretary of War in 1801. Resigning that post in 1809, he was chosen Collector of the port of Boston, until President Madison made him the US Army's senior Major-General in January 1812 in anticipation of renewed conflict with Great Britain.

Dearborn was sent to Albany, New York, reaching that place on May 4 where he was to recruit, train and organize a northern army for operations against Canada. But no sooner had he arrived than he left for Boston to supervise coastal defenses and enlist men from New England. He did not return to Albany until late July. Meanwhile, Henry Hull and his Army of the Northwest had been in western Upper Canada for over a week, hoping Dearborn would be applying pressure on Kingston, Niagara and Montreal, so British forces could not be brought to bear against him from the east. When Dearborn finally got back to Albany, he found only 1,200 untrained and ill-equipped men waiting there, and no plan for an immediate march against any of the objectives agreed to in the pre-war strategy.

Something else Dearborn found when he returned to Albany was that Secretary of War Eustis had appointed a number of new generals to work under him on the northern front. One of them, Stephen Van Rensselaer, Major-General of New York militia, was assigned command of the Niagara sector. Born on November 1, 1764, the former Lieutenant-Governor of New York was a Federalist, the head of one of the first families of New York State, but had no military experience and was against the war. He accepted the position only as a way to increase his popularity with the voters of New York when he ran again for public office. He was offered the post because at the time only New York militiamen were available for duty on the Niagara and he was their authorized commander.

In a letter to Eustis announcing his return to Albany, Dearborn queried the Secretary as to whether his command authority extended to Upper Canada, including the Niagara front. It did, but the fact that the senior officer in the United States Army did not know that did not bode well for America's success in the war. As Dearborn wondered what he really commanded, one of his posts came under attack. On July 11, five ships of the Canadian Provincial Marine fell upon Sackets Harbor on the southeast side of Lake Ontario. For two hours, the Canadian vessels fought both the American shore batteries protecting the port and an America warship, the 18-gun *Oneida*, the only US craft on the lake at the time. The British were driven off with heavy damage to their flagship and with no injury to the American defenders.

Starting on July 26, a series of orders from Washington, DC to Dearborn directed him to arrange immediate cooperation with Hull by way of some diversions against the Niagara Peninsula and Kingston, "as soon as practicable and by such operations as may be within your control." The general's strange response, even though he had no power to do so, was to arrange an armistice with the British on August 9 at the request of the commander of all British forces in Canada, Sir George Prevost. Both sides used the unauthorized truce to hurry troops and supplies to the forward areas. The Americans got the most out of the deal since the British had more experienced soldiers on the frontier, outnumbering Dearborn at Albany and Van Rensselaer on the Niagara River, and were more capable of going over to the offensive. In fact Brock, who wanted to attack Sackets Harbor—the only good anchorage the Americans had on the US side of Lake Ontario—was denied the opportunity by the impromptu ceasefire. The armistice was rescinded by the United States government, but Dearborn continued to honor it until August 19, and refused to obey Eustis' order to advance on Kingston and over the Niagara River

The weeks dragged by and although Dearborn made noises to the effect that if he were reinforced he would take Montreal and Kingston and cross the Niagara before winter, he did not stir. During the first week of October, 6,300 American troops, mostly militia, were stationed on the northern frontier. In the meantime, the British were more active. Soon after Hull surrendered at Detroit, Brock hurried east, arriving at Fort Erie, opposite Buffalo, on August 23. He was eager to sweep the enemy from the entire Niagara zone, but his hand was stayed by the defensive policy Prevost was obligated to follow. In rapid succession, the general made a tour of inspection at Kingston and then Fort George on his way to take command of the Niagara border.

Sackets Harbor, a key US naval base on Lake Ontario, came under British attack on July 11, 1812, but fought them off.

The contrast between Henry Dearborn and Isaac Brock could not have been more pronounced. While the former was lethargic and hesitant, the latter was quick, bold, confident and eager for action. Born on October 6, 1769, in St. Peter Port on the Channel Island of Guernsey, he grew to be an impressive 6'2" tall. In 1785 he joined the British Army as an Ensign, then purchased a Captain's commission and transferred to the 49th Regiment of Foot in 1791. After purchasing a Lieutenant-Colonelcy, he became commander of his regiment in 1799, accompanying it on the Helder Expedition to Holland, where he was wounded in the throat by a musket ball. In 1802, he and the 49th Foot were transferred to Canada. In 1807 he was promoted to Brigadier-General and in 1811, Major-General. That same year he was made both military and civil head of Upper Canada. His tireless efforts and energy in training and organizing the regulars and militia in Upper Canada, along with his acute strategic sense, forced William Hull's surrender at Detroit and cleared the Americans from the Old Northwest Territory.

✦ ✦ ✦

Near the end of October, Major-General Van Rensselaer was reinforced by a brigade of regulars under Brigadier-General Alexander Smyth. Born on September 14, 1767, in Ireland, Smyth emigrated to Virginia while a child, became a lawyer, and held state public office before he was appointed colonel of the newly formed Regiment of Riflemen in 1808. Without any military credentials, he got the command because of his pristine political connections. Because he had authored a drill book for the army, he was made a Brigadier General and Dearborn's Inspector General when the War of 1812 broke out. Preferring battlefield glory to tedious paper work, he got Dearborn to give him command of an infantry brigade assigned to the Niagara front. He wore his contempt for Van Rensselaer and the militia as plainly as he wore his general's insignia.

With 6,300 men under his command, Van Rensselaer determined to initiate an attack across the Niagara River. Opposing him was Brock's 1,200 regulars and militia as well as a few hundred Mohawk Indians. The British position was anchored at Fort Erie, located at the outlet of Lake Erie, opposite Buffalo, and Fort George at the mouth of the Niagara River. A central body of troops stationed at Chippawa, just above Niagara Falls, acted as a reserve. At Queenston, which lay between Fort George and Chippawa, Brock placed 300 regulars and militia as well as a single 3-pounder field piece. An 18-pounder in a small earthwork was positioned just south of the town a little way back from the river.

The American plan was an ambitious one but sound: part of the army would cross the Niagara and directly assault Queenston, cutting the Portage Road between Lake Ontario and Lake Erie. At the same time, a force of regulars would boat down from American-held Fort Niagara westward along the shore of Lake Ontario, land behind Fort George and attack its weaker landward side. The movement seemed right for the operation, since the Americans believed, wrongly as it turned out, that Brock had taken a large portion of his troops out of the theater and gone to the West.

Van Rensselaer, however, received no support for his plan from the recently arrived

Smyth, who preferred his own scheme for an American crossing of the Niagara between Fort Erie and Chippawa. Smyth would not even meet with his commander to discuss military matters. Instead, Van Rensselaer decided to attack Queenston with the troops he commanded at Lewiston on the night of October 10. The effort became farcical when the troops, in a driving rain, had to abandon the effort because the officer in charge of the boats had not readied them for the crossing. With his thoroughly disgruntled men clamoring for action, Van Rensselaer determined to try once more, this time on October 13. Again Smyth refused to join in, declaring that his men could not be ready to act until the 14th since they needed time to "rest and clean up."

The early hours of Tuesday, the 13th, were again rain-filled as 600 US assault troops moved to the river bank and looked across the wide and fast flowing Niagara, whose banks were considerably higher on the British side. In charge of the operation was Van Rensselaer's competent cousin, Colonel Solomon Van Rensselaer. With only 13 large boats available for the crossing, just about half of the American force could be transported at one time. The 350 regulars of the 13th US Infantry Regiment made up the first assault wave.

Battle of Queenston on the Niagara River on October 13, 1812, started promisingly for the Americans, but ended with a British victory.

Ten minutes after shoving off from the shore, the regulars touched the enemy bank, but not before three of their boats were carried away by the current below the landing point.

Once Colonel Rensselaer stepped ashore with the first wave, he was attacked by British Grenadiers of the 49th Foot in conjunction with some Canadian militia, supported by their 3-pounder and 18-pounder cannon. The Americans, stymied by the enemy fire, retired to the riverbank. In the storm of shot, Colonel Rensselaer was wounded, as was his second in command, Captain John E. Wool, who was injured through both his thighs.

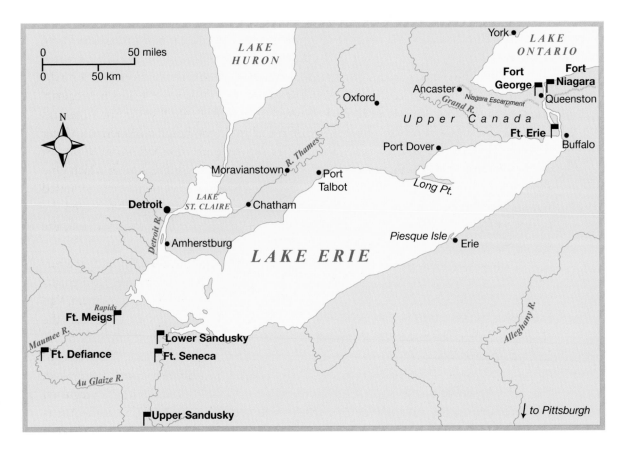

Eager to storm the heights above them, the Americans, led by Wool, who heroically ignored his wound, followed an unguarded path that brought them up a high slope from which they had a commanding view of the British position. At this moment, General Brock arrived from Fort George where the sound of the fighting at Queenston was clearly audible. As he rode toward the battle, he ordered elements of the York Militia to follow him. He also sent instructions to General Sheaffe to bring reinforcements to Queenston from Fort George and to open an artillery bombardment on Fort Niagara with the guns at Fort George. By 7:00am, he had reached the 18-pounder position and told the leader of the Light Company, 49th Foot, stationed on the nearby ridge, to go join the British troops engaged with the Americans near the river. Just after the Light Company departed, Wool and his soldiers arrived on the summit above the redoubt and rushed the gun position.

Realizing that the Americans had to be forced from the heights and the artillery emplacement retaken or the battle would be lost, Brock ordered most of the troops from the riverbank, some 190 of them, to form up for an attack on the Americans now holding the high ground. The British no sooner commenced their direct attack up the steep slope when they were forced back by heavy fire from 150 American defenders above them. Attempting to rally his men, Brock shouted, "This is the first time I have ever seen the 49th turn their backs!" Mounted, he then led them in a renewed effort. Moments later, the general was hit by two bullets—the first in his wrist, the second passing through his chest, killing him instantly.

Seeing their leader fall, the Redcoats faltered and fell back. Soon after, Brock's aide, Lieutenant-Colonel John McDonell, arrived with the York Militia. He rallied the regulars and sent 180 of them back into the attack just as their flanking party struck the American left, which was then rolled back to the edge of the cliffs. At this point, an American officer attempted to raise the white flag of surrender but Wool pulled it down. Reinforced by part of the US 6th Infantry Regiment, the two sides exchanged intense fire, during which time all the leading British officers were hit. McDonell, who like Brock before him was mounted and an easy target, was mortally wounded. Wool then ordered a charge that forced the British to retire to Queenston. Joined there by friendly forces still on the riverbank, the whole retreated further on to Vrooman's Point.

From the end of the fight for the heights at 10:00am until about 2:00pm that afternoon, the Americans fed reinforcements across the river. During this time, Lieutenant-Colonel Winfield Scott, 2nd United States Artillery Regiment, prevailed upon General Van Rensselaer to allow him to take charge of all the troops on the west shore. Suddenly the quiet was broken by a surprise attack by Iroquois Indians under their chief John Brant. Lieutenant Jared Willson, who was at the scene, was shocked by the militia's refusal to fight the native warriors. "The Indian war whoop even echoed through their camp," he recalled, "and still they could not be prevailed upon to mingle with their associates [the US regulars] in arms to oppose the inhuman foe." Panicked by the sudden Indian appearance, the Americas were thrown into confusion until Scott, exhibiting great calm, was able to restore order among them. The tribesmen were then chased away into the woods.

As the US soldiers and Indians traded sporadic shots at each other, Major-General Roger Hale Sheaffe, now successor to Brock as British commander in Upper Canada, reached Vrooman's Point with 700 regulars and militia. Intending to avoid a frontal charge on the enemy, he marched to the west and ascended the escarpment above the American left with about 1,000 whites and 300 Indians.

While the British were receiving reinforcements, 1,200 American militiamen on the east side of the Niagara refused to cross the river to the Canadian side. They stood on the principal that they were not required to leave United States territory, although fear of Indians and being shot perhaps had more to do with their refusal than constitutional scruples.

As a result, all General Van Rensselaer could do was leave the choice of retreating back over the Niagara to the officers on the other side, a task made nearly impossible by the abandonment of the boats by their cowardly crews.

With only 250 regulars and the same number of militiamen, Scott faced Sheaffe who commenced his attack at 4:00pm. As the British and Indians advanced on the Americans, two British guns raked the US right flank from the village of Queenston. At the first downhill rush of the British, the American militiamen broke and fled, while the US regulars were overwhelmed after a brief but stiff fight. Pushed to the riverbank, with no way to cross the water, the defeated Yankees had little choice but to surrender. Ignoring a hoisted white flag of surrender, the Indians kept firing at their foe until Scott stepped forward, waving a white neck cloth that caught the attention of the British, who then halted the Indian fire and accepted the American capitulation.

At Queenston, 90 American soldiers were killed, 100 wounded, and 925 taken prisoner. Since, during the last phase of the battle, Scott had less than 600 men in action it appears many of the captured never fought but merely hid until picked up by the British. Sheaffe reported his losses in the engagement at 14 killed, 77 wounded, and 21 missing.

Uniform of Major-General Isaac Brock shows the hole made by the fateful bullet that pierced his chest during the battle of Queenston.

American
soldiers
tumble off
the heights
during fierce
fighting at
the battle of
Queenston.

Dearborn condemned Rensselaer's defeat as "the most mortifying unexpected event." He accepted the New Yorker's resignation and gave the command of the Niagara front to Smyth, not knowing how much the latter's non-cooperation had helped compromise the entire venture. On the British side, the effects of the victory at Queenston halted any talk of not being able to defend Canada from the United States, and saw a dramatic increase in the number of volunteering Canadian militiamen, who not only turned out in greater numbers but who remained on active duty for a considerable time.

Reacting to the debacle at Queenston, Dearborn pressed the newly elevated commander of the Army of the Center, Smyth, to lead an invasion of Canada along the Niagara border, assuring the Irishman that a diversionary effort in the Lake Champlain area would be mounted to aid him. Smyth had only 4,000 half-trained poorly equipped regulars, and his militia contingent had been leaving him in droves. Nevertheless, he did intend to make a move.

Smyth's plan for an attack on Canada, even though the season was late, encompassed a crossing at the southern end of the Niagara with 3,000 men. The operation began on

November 28 when a force under Colonel William H. Winder, and another led by Lieutenant-Colonel Charles G. Boerstler, passed over the river. Winder was to take the enemy
batteries on the opposite shore and Boerstler was to block any British reinforcements from
moving south from Chippawa and Fort George. Once these objectives were accomplished,
Smyth's main force was to leave Buffalo and head north to enter Winder and Boerstler's
bridgehead.

In the event, Winder was successful in taking the enemy guns but lost a detachment
of his men to superior British numbers when they strayed too close to Fort Erie. Boerstler
lost a few boats to artillery fire as he was crossing, causing him to lose his nerve and row
back to the American bank. Unsupported, Winder was forced to withdraw back to the east
shore. In the meantime, Smyth's main body took to boats and slowly got under way, so
slowly in fact that their part of the assault was aborted because of the long delay and the
suspicion that any surprise the attack might have achieved was by then long gone. Soon
thereafter the Niagara Front went into winter hibernation.

✦   ✦   ✦

Of the three military fronts opened up in 1812, the Lake Champlain theater had been relatively peaceful. This was strange considering this area was the natural jumping off point
for any offensive against the vital regions of both the United States and Canada; that is,
Albany and Montreal. Here, control of Lake Champlain was key to any advance going
north or south for logistical reasons. For an American army advancing on Montreal, or a
British army going for Albany, the attackers would have to go by foot since the Richelieu
River was not only well guarded, but its navigation was treacherous due to its rapids. The
control of Lake Champlain was vital and thus the Americans established a base at Plattsburg, New York.

In September, Brigadier-General Joseph Bloomfield, who was also Governor of
New Jersey, took command of the Northern Army on the Lake Champlain front. By
November he favored an attack on Montreal with his force of 3,500 regulars and 2,500
militiamen. Bloomfield planned to advance into Canada on the 16th. After Bloomfield fell
ill, Dearborn, who had just arrived in camp, took charge and moved to the border. At this
point, Colonel Zebulon Pike was detached to attack a British advanced post on the Lacolle
River, a tributary of the Richelieu. After a confused firefight, the British withdrew and Pike
and his men returned to camp. Pike's little skirmish would be the most intense action of
Dearborn's advance. Dearborn had to abort his intention of crossing into Canada when
most of his militiamen refused to accompany him. Furthermore, the expected naval support, which would have allowed an assault on Isle aux Noix—the armed post guarding the
Richelieu River—never appeared. Dearborn had no choice but to return to Plattsburg and
enter winter quarters, which the army did on November 22.

As the "Hero of the West" since his victory at Tippecanoe the year before, William
Henry Harrison was made a Brigadier-General in the United States Army in August 1812,
and as the new commander of the Army of the Northwest, he was given a free hand in

the effort to recover Detroit. He was born in Charles City County, Virginia, on February 22, 1773. He began to study medicine but in 1791 became an Ensign in the United States Army and served as an aide to General Anthony Wayne. He rose to the rank of Captain, but again changed careers in 1798 to go into politics, being appointed in 1800, at the age of 27, as Governor of the Indiana Territory.

Assuring the US government that he would take back Detroit before winter, he set off with almost 10,000 men in four columns in late September for the Grand Rapids on the Maumee River. As they advanced, the American troop columns were widely separated and moved beyond supporting distance. Taking advantage of this, Colonel Proctor, at Detroit, sent his trusted subordinate, Adam Muir, now a Brevet-Major, with 500 regulars and militiamen, 500 Indians, and a few light artillery pieces up the Maumee River, intending to ambush part of Harrison's force under Brigadier General James Winchester. The Americans got wind of the plot and took up a defensive position. Outnumbered and running low of supplies, Muir was forced to withdraw, but he had accomplished part of his assignment by slowing Winchester to a crawl out of fear of another trap.

For the next two months it rained constantly, turning the area into ribbons of mud, halting the movement of supplies to Harrison's army and causing it great hunger. In addition, the death rate among the men climbed and desertion became rampant. On December 20, Harrison ordered Winchester to move to the Grand Rapids on the Maumee River and establish an advanced base for the final march on Detroit, and ultimately Fort Malden in Upper Canada. At the same time, however, while professing to be eager to continue his campaign even during the wretched winter season, Harrison slyly suggested to President Madison that the objects of the campaign would be easier obtained in May of the next year when the weather was better and ships could be built on Lake Erie to support his army. Clearly, the general was trying to shift the blame for his faltering western effort to the politicians in Washington. The Madison administration sidestepped this by leaving the choice to Harrison as to whether to continue his advance to Detroit. On January 6, 1813, Harrison sent the Secretary of War a letter admitting it would be best to suspend his winter operations. Unfortunately, the matter would not end there.

The end of 1812 had come and with it a very disappointing first six months of war for the United States. Battles and territory had been lost, a few generals who should never have been given the responsibility of waging war were gone, but plenty more like them remained. Secretary of War William Eustis was forced to resign his post on December 3, 1812, after the loss of Detroit and the defeat at Queenston. In 1814 he was appointed US Ambassador to the Netherlands, and in 1823 Governor of Massachusetts, dying in that office on February 6, 1825. He had proved untrained and unsuited to making military decisions and carrying them through. It was hoped that in 1813 the nation could find a leader who could.

USS Constitution, *a 44-gun frigate, launched in 1797 and dubbed "Old Ironsides." Painting by Antonio Jacobsen.*

CHAPTER FOUR

American Success at Sea

———————————— ❧❧❧ ————————————

"Now lads," the stern faced captain of the USS *President* began as he addressed his crew, "we have got something to do that will shake the rust from our jackets. War is declared! We shall have another dash at our old enemies." Thus, on June 21, 1812, Commodore John Rodgers, United States Navy, announced to his men that war existed between their country and Great Britain. To the spontaneous cheers of the *President's* complement, he promised that the United States would teach John Bull a lesson, and that he expected every man who sailed with him to spare no effort in administrating that lesson.

A Marylander, Rodgers was born on July 11, 1772. For 11 years, he was part of the merchant marine before joining the fledging United States Navy in 1798 as a lieutenant. In America's Quasi-War with France he saw action, most notably during the famous 1799 sea encounter between the *Constellation* and the French frigate *L'Insurgent*. That same year, he was promoted to captain. He left the navy in 1801 for the merchant marine service.

In 1802, Rodgers returned to duty and commanded the light frigate USS *Adams*, then the USS *Constitution* during the war against the Barbary pirates. In 1805, as *de facto* leader of all US warships in the Mediterranean, he was able to conclude peace treaties with Tripoli and Tunis, bringing the Barbary conflict to a close. He next led the US Navy's New York station and then, just before the war with Britain, the nation's northern squadron. Although a harsh disciplinarian, he was no martinet and was a master when it came to managing a warship.

With the outbreak of war, the US Navy Department ordered Rodgers to join with Commodore Stephen Decatur's three warships which had just come north from Norfolk, Virginia, at Sandy Hook, New Jersey. Decatur, born in Maryland on January 5, 1779, was renowned for his part in the war against Tripoli. In 1798, he joined the navy as a midshipman. During the Barbary War, as a lieutenant, Decatur led an American raiding party that destroyed the USS *Philadelphia* which had been captured by the pirates of Tripoli; later in the same year, he led an attack on that city's defenses. The years leading up to the conflict with Britain found Decatur promoted to captain and tasked with patrolling the nation's territorial waters. Decatur exemplified the heroic warrior, but was also cursed with a hair-trigger temper when it came to matters of personal honor and prerogatives. He was also able of being utterly ruthless toward those who did not measure up to his standards, or stood in the way of his ambition.

With conflict between America and Great Britain imminent, the US Secretary of the Navy, Paul Hamilton, consulted Rodgers and Decatur for their ideas regarding naval strategy. Rodgers favored dispersion of the ships, with the proviso that in the right circumstances all the frigates, and at times the entire fleet, should be assembled as a single strike force for particular missions. Decatur had a similar take on the matter but saw no reason why more than one, or at most a pair of frigates, should be sent out on any one long-range commerce raid.

Legendary US naval commander Stephen Decatur enjoyed his own victory over HMS Macedonian *in October 1812.*

While Rodgers and Decatur thirsted to "annoy" the British by attacking their merchantmen and keeping their warships running all over the ocean looking for the fast, phantom-like American frigates, the Secretary of the Navy was less sanguine about the outcome of the naval war. After Rodgers and Decatur put to sea in late June 1812, the Secretary noted his officers' confidence in their ability to beat the British, but wrote, "When I reflect on the overwhelming force of our enemy my heart swells almost to bursting, and all the consolation I have is, that in falling they [the American ships and crews] will fall nobly."

Paul Hamilton was born October 16, 1762, in South Carolina. He fought as a militiaman in the Revolutionary War battles in the South. He became governor of the Palmetto State in 1804, going on to become Madison's Secretary of the Navy in 1809, despite the fact that other than being a Republican he possessed no qualifications for the job. After war was declared, he failed to define a clear strategy for the Navy, vacillating between keeping the ships concentrated close to the American coast to protect US merchant vessels, having them hide in port to prevent their destruction by the Royal Navy, and ranging the oceans in ones or twos to ravage enemy trade. Like his counterpart, William Eustis in the War Department, Hamilton was out of his depth running a military machine. Fortunately for the country, his subordinates at sea knew how to fight their ships and operate independently from the bureaucrats in Washington.

✦ ✦ ✦

"If, on your way thither," enjoined the letter from Secretary Hamilton to the Captain of the USS *Constitution*, "you shall fall in with an enemy vessel, you will be guided in your proceeding by your own judgment, bearing in mind however, that you are not, voluntarily, to encounter a force superior to your own." This missive, written on July 3, was received onboard the American frigate as it was making its way from Chesapeake Bay to the sea. When war between America and Britain was declared, the 44-gun

Connecticut-born Isaac Hull, commander of the USS Constitution *during a string of victorious naval combats in 1812. Portrait by Gilbert Stuart in 1807.*

Constitution was undergoing refitting at the Washington Navy Yard, and she and her captain, Isaac Hull, were ordered to join Rodgers and Decatur at New York as quickly as possible. Hamilton's cautionary message must have irked the *Constitution's* skipper since he was an experienced sailor and roaring for a fight.

Isaac Hull was a Connecticut Yankee born on March 9, 1773. Already a qualified ship's master, he joined the US Navy in 1798, rising to first lieutenant on the USS *Constitution*. He served on her during the Quasi-War. After commanding several smaller warships in the Navy, he gained his captaincy as a result of his prior command assignments and participation in the war with Tripoli. Prior to the struggle against Britain, he held command of the frigates *Chesapeake* and *President* before taking over *Constitution* in 1810. Now, during that hot July of 1812, the bold and testy Hull raced north to combine with

USS Constitution *escaping from British warships in July 1812. Becalmed, she had to be towed away before the pursuing vessels. Painting by J.O. Davidson.*

the other American frigates in a mission not yet clearly defined.

On July 16, at Egg Harbor, near present day Atlantic City, New Jersey, the *Constitution's* lookouts sighted four ships far off to the north and close to the shore. Hull headed for the nearest stranger to ascertain its nationality. By 10:30pm, after a two-hour approach, the American was certain the mystery vessel was British. Hull hauled off into the wind to the south and east and prepared to do battle the next day. The British ship followed. He confidently declared to his officers that they could "flog" the foe in two and a half hours.

The predawn light revealed to the crew of the US frigate that they were being dogged by not only the British ship spotted the day before but an enemy squadron consisting of the *Guerriere, Shannon, Belvidera, Aeolus,* and *Africa,* strung out in line about six to ten miles astern of the American. The nearest British craft, HMS *Guerriere,* under Captain James R. Dacres, was closing fast until her chief, fearing he had stumbled into the American squadron led by John Rodgers instead of his own comrades, veered off—wasting 10 minutes—before returning to the pursuit. But Dacres' momentary lapse was cancelled out when the wind fell completely away from *Constitution's* sails while continuing to fill those of the British. The American slowed so much that her bow started to turn toward her pursers! Hull immediately ordered all the ship's boats lowered to tow *Constitution* into the wind toward the south.

Fierce broadsides unleashed in the 25-minute battle between the USS Constitution *and HMS* Guerriere *in August 1812, chopping down one of the masts of the British vessel.*

HMS *Shannon* overtook the *Guerriere* in the pursuit, but like the *Constitution,* was suddenly becalmed and had to deploy oar-driven longboats in the same fashion. Meantime, apertures in the *Constitution's* aft were made so that four of her 24-pounder guns could fire at the enemy. At 7:00am, Hull fired one of these pieces at the frigates on his tail. No American or British return fire struck its mark, but with HMS *Shannon* leading the pack, it appeared that the US vessel was doomed. In fact, Captain Philip B.V. Broke, in charge of the squadron and commander of the *Shannon*, was so confident of the American's capture that he had earlier that morning selected an officer and crew to man what he was certain would be his prize before the day was out.

About to turn his ship broadside to engage the entire force descending on his ship, Hull was alerted to a maneuver by one of his officers that saved the Americans. The technique referred to as kedging called for rowing out an anchor ahead of the ship on a long line, dropping it, and then having the crew haul it in to move the ship forward. If done correctly, speeds of up to three knots could be achieved. A launch and cutter were sent ahead of the ship with two anchors and two lines which were worked alternately. The distance between *Constitution* and her hunters started to widen, but not before the *Guerriere* was able to deliver an ineffective volley at "Old Ironsides."

The race over the water between the opposing warships continued all day with Hull dumping drinking water from the hold to lighten his ship. Meanwhile, another British frigate, HMS *Belvidera,* towed by ten longboats, converged on the American prey hoping to send the latter a broadside strong enough to slow the Yankee's progress so the rest of *Belvidera's* comrades could catch up. The *Constitution* replied with its own fire and one round shot scattered a group of British officers standing on *Belvidera's* forecastle, but both sides' long-range gunnery had little effect. The chase continued all night.

July 18 dawned with enemy frigates on *Constitution's* lee bow, beam, and eastward of her. In addition, a British capital ship, brig, and schooner trailed two miles behind. After avoiding being cut off by *Belvidera*, and soon thereafter by the frigate HMS *Aeolus*, the American started to pull away from her followers using another unique sailing trick: spraying water on the sails to keep them wet and tight and thus better able to catch the wind. As the hunted and the hunters continued throughout the day, they came upon a single US merchantman. One of the British frigates raised an American flag in order to deceive and capture her. Seeing this, Hull responded by hoisting a British flag, thus scaring the freighter away from the scene.

By 2:00pm the United States man-of-war was making over 12 knots before a strengthening wind, giving her an eight-mile lead. July 19 saw the British give up the chase. *Constitution's* crew had been at general quarters for 60 continuous hours and were exhausted by their ordeal. On the 26th, the *Constitution* entered Boston harbor. Hull sent communications to Hamilton explaining that due to the presence of a superior number of enemy warships in the area, it had been impossible to obey his orders to reach New York, and that he wished to put to sea again as soon as possible to avoid being penned in Boston harbor by the Royal Navy.

Final moment of the battle between the USS Constitution *and HMS* Guerriere *as the British ship is completely crippled and her crew forced to surrender.*

✦ ✦ ✦

Besides the USS *Constitution*, the start of war saw another American warship not ready for action. The USS *Essex*, a 32-gun frigate under Captain David Porter, was undergoing repairs at the New York Navy Yard in Brooklyn. Porter put to sea on July 3rd, just one day after he was promoted captain; his orders were to join with Rodgers as soon as possible. The Massachusetts native, born on February 1, 1780, entered the navy in 1798, served in the Quasi-War as well as the fight against Tripoli, going on to command the US naval forces at New Orleans. In 1811, he was assigned master of the *Essex*.

Failing to find Rodgers off Sandy Hook, Porter reverted to his contingency orders, which directed him to patrol between Bermuda and Newfoundland's Grand Banks. On July 11, he spotted an enemy convoy of seven transports escorted by a lone frigate. He quickly captured the rearmost carrier with its crew and 197 soldiers on board, and waited for the British warship to engage him. To Porter's surprise, the enemy frigate, HMS *Minerva*, chose not to do so but instead gathered the rest of the convoy around her and proceeded on. Porter felt he could not fight the entire group of enemy ships (the transports were armed) and so allowed the British to go unmolested. Regardless, Porter had made the first capture of an opposing ship in the War of 1812. Over the next 39 days he would take eight more prizes. On August 13, the *Essex* scored another first by defeating, in eight minutes, the 18-gun British sloop *Alert*, the first time a British man-of-war struck her colors to an American. In early September, Porter returned to the Delaware River.

✦   ✦   ✦

While Porter made the most of his cruise, and Hull made his daring escape from the British Halifax Squadron, Rodgers and Decatur embarked on a hunt for a reportedly huge enemy convoy sailing from Jamaica to England. On this futile 70-day mission, which saw them sail from the United States to near the English Channel, then to the Azores, then Boston, they captured nine stray British merchantmen and privateers, and recaptured an American ship, but failed to locate the intended prize. For Rodgers and Decatur, the first months of the war were barren of any significant results. Rodgers was especially bitter at a missed opportunity to capture an enemy frigate that presented itself at the very beginning of his cruise.

On June 23, two days after leaving New York and 100 miles southwest of Nantucket Sound, Rodgers' little fleet stumbled upon HMS *Belvidera* under Captain Richard Byron. The 36-gun English frigate was part of the British North American Squadron based at Halifax. When the Americans were six miles away, Byron realized who was approaching him and that war with the United States had most likely been declared. He sailed for the northeast with Rodgers' USS *President* in hot pursuit, the other American ships falling well behind. Eight hours after the first sighting, Rodgers' ship opened fire, at half a mile distance, with her two starboard bow chaser cannon hitting the British craft in the rudder cover and one of her guns.

The two ships exchanged fire for a few minutes until one of the Yankee chase guns exploded, breaking Rodgers' leg and shattering the main and forecastle decks, killing or wounding 14 American crewmen. To slow the enemy down, Rodgers swung his ship to the right and fired a broadside in hopes of so damaging *Belvidera's* rigging that she would be crippled and captured. But the American fire had little effect, and maneuvers to cut off the British vessel proved to no avail. Coming up to pointblank range a little later, and not drawing alongside his enemy but instead moving to the right and firing another broadside, did not stop Byron either. As the chase continued, the British captain lightened his ship by dumping water and other items over the side. He slowly started to outdistance his pursuers, and the American gave up the race. The British frigate entered Halifax harbor on June 27 after capturing three surprised American merchantmen along the way.

Losses on the *President* were three killed and 19 wounded; *Belvidera* lost two killed and 22 injured. Decatur summed up the entire humiliating affair when he recorded that "We have lost the *Belvidera;* [she] should have been ours." The first armed clash of the War of 1812 had been fought, and for the American Navy it had been a lost opportunity.

✦ ✦ ✦

On August 2, USS *Constitution* weighed anchor and left Boston harbor, planning to join USS *President*. She cruised northeast along the coast of Maine and then headed for Newfoundland, taking station off the Gulf of St. Lawrence to intercept enemy ships bound for Halifax and Quebec. On the 19th her commander, Isaac Hull, spotted HMS *Guerriere*, detached from Broke's flotilla and ordered for duty at Halifax. Hull immediately raced toward her. British Captain James R. Dacres saw the American ship at the same time and eagerly prepared to engage. Dacres was born on August 22, 1788. The son of a Royal Navy admiral, he had commanded two warships prior to being named in 1811 master of the *Guerriere*—a captured French frigate. Prior to the war he had been especially active in recovering British deserters from US merchant ships. After war was declared, he reputedly issued a challenge to any and all American frigates to meet him in one-to-one combat.

As the two warships closed the range between them, *Constitution* held the weather gauge. This allowed her to better maneuver than her opponent, giving her the opportunity to either haul away and avoid a fight, or use the wind to directly make for the enemy. That posed its own risks since a direct approach exposed the oncoming ship to the other's full broadside while unable to respond with return fire. Nevertheless, Hull chose to attack head-on.

As *Constitution* sped forward, she was met by several of *Guerriere's* broadsides, which fell too short or too high. Hull ordered more sail put on so he could more rapidly bring *Constitution* right alongside her opponent. The stern-most guns from the British vessel started to fire at the fast approaching adversary, cutting down several of the American crew. At 6:00pm, *Constitution* drew alongside her opponent and loosed a shattering starboard broadside, fired from double-shotted cannon, into the deck and gun ports of the enemy frigate. The impact shook the British ship "as though she had received the shock of an earthquake." Seconds later, *Guerriere's* mizzenmast crashed into the water.

Hull ordered his ship to forge ahead of the stricken enemy, then turned hard to port in order to cross her bow. *Guerriere* tried to turn with *Constitution*, but her fallen mizzenmast, dragging in the sea, slowed her too much to match *Constitution's* speed. The Yankee completed her maneuver and poured two massive broadsides into the bow of the British vessel, mowing down men and damaging her remaining masts. At this time, the *Guerriere's* bowsprit and jibboom became entangled in *Constitution's* mizzenmast rigging. Both crews, in reaction, prepared to board each other's ship or repulse boarders. As the crews gathered on deck, United States Marines firing down from their ship's mizzenmast hit enemy sailors below. One of them was Dacres who was wounded in the back. Then *Guerriere's* mainmast toppled over, and Hull moved away from his crippled enemy.

For the next half hour, the *Constitution* kept her distance and affected battle repairs, while the *Guerriere* rolled "like a log in the trough of the sea," her main deck awash with water, having suffered 30 holes punched below her waterline. After coming forward and standing across *Guerriere's* bow, Hull sent a boat over, demanding her surrender. Dacres came aboard *Constitution* to formally give up, and in a voice of wonderment exclaimed to Hull, "Your men are a set of tigers."

The sea battle, 600 miles from Boston, had lasted just 25 minutes. American losses were seven dead and seven wounded; the British sustained 15 dead and 62 wounded, with 25 more missing. The British ship was a total wreck and could not be safely towed. "Old Ironsides" was not hulled by a single shot. Next day the Americans set *Guerriere* ablaze with explosives, sinking her. Hull then set a course for Boston harbor, reaching there on August 29.

✦ ✦ ✦

Commodore William Bainbridge took over from Hull as commander of USS Constitution. *Portrait by Gilbert Stuart in 1813.*

After reaching Boston, Hull was transferred from the *Constitution* to command the Navy Yard there, and William Bainbridge was assigned the stewardship of the *Constitution* in his place. Born May 7, 1774, in Princeton, New Jersey, he joined the US Navy in 1798 as a lieutenant. He commanded a schooner in the Caribbean that year but was forced to surrender his ship to the French during the Quasi-War. The impetuous and exacting officer's hard luck did not change when he was made to use his next command, USS *George Washington,* as a courier for the Ottoman Turks. The nadir of his career occurred in 1803 when he ran his latest charge, USS *Philadelphia,* aground, allowing it to be captured by the Bey of Tripoli. He spent the next 19 months a prisoner.

Bainbridge was never blamed for the mishaps that befell his ships in the early 1800s, and due to his political influence was promoted captain and served as commandant of the Boston Navy Yard. In 1812, after lobbying for command of one of the navy's big frigates, his politicking got him command of *Constitution*. Imbued with a killer's instinct and boastful drive, he proved an adequate if not a brilliant naval officer.

Constitution's victory over *Guerriere* prompted Secretary of the Navy Hamilton to let loose Stephen Decatur and his USS *United States* on a cruise to the Canary Islands to raid British shipping. Decatur hoped to also tangle with a British frigate and equal Hull's success over the *Guerriere*. He got his chance on October 25, 1812.

On that date, halfway between the Azores and the Cape Verde Islands, Decatur spotted HMS *Macedonian*, a 38-gun frigate with 18-pounders, under the leadership of Captain John S. Carden. Born on August 15, 1771, Carden, already a veteran sailor, had been badly wounded at the battle of the Glorious First of June. Through 1809 he commanded four warships in the contest against Napoleon, gaining command of the *Macedonian* in 1810. In late September 1812, after completing convoy duty near Madeira, he was freed to sweep the western Atlantic for French and American shipping.

Spotting each other at a distance of three miles, the two warships closed the range steadily, passing one another on opposite tracts. As the vessels ran past, *United States* let off a broadside at her British counterpart, but all the 24-pounder cannon balls fell short. Carden turned in pursuit, but the resulting long angling approach to his target put him under brutal American fire from guns which out-ranged his own.

A half hour into the battle, the British ship came within 100 yards of its foe, but by then all *Macedonian*'s topmasts were shot away, and the starboard close-in fighting carronades were disabled. The American crossed *Macedonian*'s bow and, without firing a shot, retired a short distance to affect minor repairs. Soon the mizzenmast of the Royal Navy ship collapsed and she, as her captain later wrote, looked like "a perfect wreck, an unmanageable log." An hour later, *United States* returned and took up a raking position as the *Macedonian* hauled down her colors.

Macedonian lost 43 killed and 61 wounded; the Americans killed and wounded were seven and five, respectively. Both ships had fired over 1,200 rounds each, the British vessel receiving 95 hits, the American only five. Decatur was able to sail his capture to New London, receiving the nation's thanks as well as $30,000 in prize money for his feat.

✦ ✦ ✦

After leaving Boston on October 26, William Bainbridge sailed to the coast of Brazil in USS *Constitution*, hoping to meet up with the *Essex*. On December 29, 30 miles offshore near Sao Salvador, Bainbridge encountered HMS *Java*, which immediately made for the US frigate.

Captain Henry Lambert was *Java*'s skipper, and when he encountered *Constitution* he was headed for Bombay. Lambert had joined the Royal Navy in 1795, made lieutenant in 1801 and spent his first eight years in that service in the Mediterranean Sea and Indian Ocean. He commanded three other warships before coming to the *Java* in 1812

Four miles from his opponent, Bainbridge veered away, fearing he was too close to Brazil's neutral shore. Lambert gave chase, realizing his was the faster ship, and also held the weather gauge, which would normally give him the advantage in single ship-to-ship combat. As the two came alongside each other, the American fired a broadside, but the British ship did not answer and tried to use her speed to cross the *Constitution*'s bow and then rake her. Increasing *Constitution's* speed, Bainbridge thwarted the enemy move. The two craft then commenced exchanging repeated thunderous broadsides.

Bainbridge was at first hit in the left hip by a musket ball, then his leg was badly torn by a piece of flying iron, but he refused to relinquish command. For the next two hours, the frigates fought it out until *Java*, having lost most of her running rigging, could barely maneuver. Bainbridge seized his advantage, and moved to rake his opponent's stern with two powerful broadsides. Clearly losing the artillery contest, Lambert sought to bring his ship closer in order to board his enemy. *Java's* main topmast and foremast were then shot away, and soon after Lambert was critically wounded by a musket ball through the chest.

With her guns silent, and her mizzenmast gone, *Java* still refused to surrender. *Constitution*, which had moved away to repair her own damage, came back after an hour ready to finish off her foe. She moved in position to rake the *Java's* bow. Seeing the impending holocaust about to unfold, *Java's* crew took down her colors and gave up. She had lost 57 killed and 83 wounded; the American loss was nine killed and 26 wounded. Lambert died January 4, 1813 from his injuries. Thus ended the most brutal and bloody frigate-to-frigate action of the entire war.

Close-up of gundecks of USS Constitution.

USS Constitution, *the world's oldest floating commissioned naval vessel, now a museum ship anchored at the Charlestown Navy Yard Pier in Boston.*

While warships of the United States Navy were racking up high seas victories and filling the nation with pride, enterprising American businessmen were counting up profits from privateering and filling their pockets with money. Some of the earliest successes, and a perfect example of the practice, came from a group of Baltimore entrepreneurs who outfitted a schooner, the *Rosie,* mounting 10 cannon, under legendary Revolutionary War hero Joshua Barney. Starting on July 11, and for the next 90 days, Barney and the *Rosie* captured 18 British merchantmen worth $1.5 million.

"The Public will learn," lamented the *London Times* on March 13, 1813, "that a third British frigate has struck its flag to an American . . . three frigates! Anyone who predicted such a result in an American war this time last year would have been treated as a madman or a traitor." British commentators pondered whether the enemy had a secret weapon; that is, better gunpowder or ships-of-the-line disguised as frigates. Some pointed out, correctly, that American success was due to "the superior strength of their vessels, their picked crews, their practiced and murderous mode of firing, and the almost uniform advantage they have in sailing."

In December 1812, USS Constitution *clashes with and defeats HMS* Java *off the coast of Brazil. Painting by CR Patterson.*

The British Admiralty sought to redress the imbalance between its frigates and those of the enemy by ordering its frigates not to engage the bigger United States vessels alone, but wait until a capital ship arrived on the scene. More gunnery practice was also urged.

Concerning the rash of American privateer activity, the British intended to establish a "wooden wall" off the coast of the United States to prevent those "pirates" from putting out to sea and threatening His Majesty's ocean-going commerce. But this would take both time and more ships, which were not yet available for the task.

If the war at sea had not gone according to British plans in 1812, that year had seen remarkable success for their forces on land, considering the limited resources available to the British in North America. There was no question that the United States would launch new attacks on Canada in 1813, but would America be more successful in that endeavor in the coming year than she had been in the one preceding?

CHAPTER FIVE

Battle for the Lakes

"THE OFFICERS OF THE [PROVINCIAL] MARINE APPEAR TO BE DESTITUTE OF ALL energy and spirit," was the evaluation of a report to Sir George Prevost regarding the action fought on November 10, 1812, at Kingston harbor between US and British naval forces on Lake Ontario. That engagement, in which each side suffered only one killed and a few wounded, secured American control of the lake for the remainder of the navigation season. The American attack, led by Commodore Isaac Chauncey, on Kingston, located at the point where the St. Lawrence River enters Lake Ontario, was long overdue, since the war had been in progress for ten weeks and control of the Great Lakes was vital for US operations against the Canadian border.

The Connecticut-born sailor, born on February 20, 1772, joined the US Navy in 1798 and participated in the Quasi-War as a 1st Lieutenant. His service in the war against the Barbary pirates earned him a captain's rank, and he was later head of the New York Navy Yard. In September 1812, based on his proven administrative ability, he was given command of US naval forces on Lakes Erie and Ontario. He transformed the village of Sackets Harbor (spelled Sackett's at the time) into America's main naval base on the Great Lakes, complete with shipbuilding and maintenance facilities. By late fall, he had supplemented the brig *Oneida*, sporting 18 32-pound short-range carronades, with four more armed schooners.

During the War of 1812, control of the Great Lakes rested with the side with the largest, most heavily armed ships. When Chauncey seized the initiative early in November, his target was the Canadian Provincial Marine's most powerful vessel, the corvette HMS *Royal George*, armed with 20 32-pounder carronades. Neutralizing her would give America dominance over Lake Ontario, thus cutting Upper Canada off from men and material, which could only flow to it along the St. Lawrence River via Montreal.

On November 10, Chauncey sailed from Sackets Harbor with the *Oneida* and six schooners, armed with a total of 63 cannon, seeking the six British ships opposing them on the lake, carrying a total of 106 guns. After destroying an enemy schooner, the US flotilla sighted *Royal George* and followed her into Kingston harbor. For two hours they exchanged long-range fire, with little damage inflicted on either side, before the Americans broke off the action. Although tactically inconclusive, the battle closed Kingston's port to British shipping, forcing the Provincial Marine's units to disperse to other havens. On November 26, Chauncey's advantage over the British increased with the launching of the corvette USS *Madison*, armed with 24 32-pounder carronades, built at Sackets Harbor in only 45 days.

Captain James Lucas Yeo of the Royal Navy was given command of British operations on the inland waters in North America in 1813.

The American success at Kingston prompted the British Admiralty to take over conduct of naval operations on the inland waters, assigning Captain James Lucas Yeo of the Royal Navy to the job. The 30-year-old veteran, born October 7, 1782, joined the navy as a lieutenant in 1797, and made captain in 1807. His varied accomplishments included command of warships and amphibious expeditions, until his appointment on March 19, 1813 to North America. Yeo opened shipyards at Kingston and York.

At this time, Marylander Jessie Duncan Elliott, a lieutenant in the US Navy, was tasked with establishing a naval station at Black Rock, on the Niagara River just north of Buffalo, New York. Further west on Lake Erie's south shore, 80 miles west of Black Rock, Presque Isle was being made ready as a naval base in lieu of Fort Erie, which was still in British hands.

To command the American naval presence on Lake Erie under Chauncey, Rhode Island native Oliver Hazard Perry was picked in February 1813. At the age of 17 he had been made a navy lieutenant; only five years later, he was building gunboats for the US government. Ordered to Presque Isle to construct two brigs, Perry arrived at that barren site on March 13, 1813. He remained seriously short of men and material, and the US positions at Presque Isle and Black Rock were easy prey for the forces of Lieutenant Robert Heriot Barclay.

The Scottish Barclay joined the Royal Navy in 1787 and served as acting lieutenant at the battle of Trafalgar. He lost his left arm in 1809 fighting the French. Transferring to the North American station, he was made naval commander on Lake Erie. Barclay was dissatisfied with the personnel manning his ships, composed of disgruntled Provincial Marine members and soldiers. He detested the staff Yeo had assigned him, who Barclay claimed were "the most worthless Characters that came from England." More concerned over the strength and effectiveness of his Lake Ontario squadron, Yeo did little to adequately reinforce Barclay's weak naval contingent.

✦ ✦ ✦

"Montreal is the principal commercial city in the Canadas," wrote George Prevost to the British Prime Minister on May 18, 1812, "and in the event of War, would become the first object of attack." He went on to affirm that "Quebec is the only permanent Fortress in the Canadas —it is the key to the whole and must be maintained." Thus, did the man responsible for safeguarding British North America succinctly indicate the two cornerstones upon which the defense of Canada rested during the War of 1812.

At 44 years old, Lieutenant General Sir George Prevost assumed his position as civil and military head of Canada in September 1811. Joining the British Army in 1779, he was a Brigadier-General by 1798. Prevost commanded troops in the West Indies, including Dominica, which he successfully defended against the French in 1805. In addition to his

At the age of 22, Rhode Island native Oliver Hazard Perry was ordered to command the American naval presence on Lake Erie in February 1813.

military record, he performed well as a civil administrator of St. Lucia, Dominica and Nova Scotia. In 1811, he was made Lieutenant-General. With a background of military and political achievement, Prevost seemed the perfect choice to govern the Canadian colonies. Modern historians are divided over Prevost's generalship, some calling it timid and indecisive, others stating he was merely defense-minded. Whatever it was, Prevost continued the struggle with the United States in 1813 by following a defensive policy.

While Sir George clung to a passive strategy, the new US Secretary of War, John Armstrong, planned to take offensive action in the east. Armstrong's scheme, as amended by Dearborn and Chauncey, provided for the movement of 1,700 troops from Sackets Harbor, escorted by the fleet, to attack York. Then, in conjunction with 3,000 men from Buffalo, Forts George and Erie on the Niagara River would be taken. Finally, the combined force would move on to Kingston, thus blocking the main supply artery along the St. Lawrence River from Lower to Upper Canada. York was made the initial target because the capture of the enemy ships reported there, in addition to its naval facilities, would give control of Lake Ontario to the Americans.

York—now modern Toronto and capital of Upper Canada—was the home of 500 souls. Its defenses consisted of a two-story blockhouse surrounded by a wooden stockade at its eastern end. To the west, more than a mile from the blockhouse and fronting the lakeshore, was situated one battery at the mouth of Garrison Creek, a second next to the Lieutenant Governor's house, a third, named the Half-Moon Battery, 400 yards from the Governor's residence, and the Western Battery 300 yards farther on. The town's ammunition was stored in Fort York, a little to the west of the Governor's mansion. The York garrison at the time of the American attack was 300 regulars, 350 militia and 50 Indians.

Sir Roger Hale Sheaffe, civil and military head of Upper Canada, was at York at the time of the American attack. A brave but cautious general, his leadership style did not inspire his subordinates or superiors. Chauncey's squadron of 14 ships, mounting 83 cannon and carrying 1,700 US regulars and volunteers, sailed from Sackets Harbor on April 25, 1813. Brigadier-General Zebulon Montgomery Pike—a promising military commander—laid out the plan for the assault on York. He explained that Major Benjamin Forsyth's Rifle Regiment would be the first to land on the beach, and then act as a protective screen for the first wave of infantry coming ashore. After the entire amphibious corps landed, it would form column, covered on the flanks by the riflemen, and march east against the enemy artillery positions. Pike issued orders that all civilian property must be respected and that any soldier "guilty of plundering, if convicted, be punished with death." Pike, not Dearborn—who was ill—led the mission.

At 7:00am, April 27, men of the US Rifle Regiment took to small boats for the run to shore—no more than 300 men could be moved to the landing area at a time. The American plan was to land in clear fields just west of Fort York, but strong winds pushed the boats two miles further west to a wooded coast, which afforded the defenders cover. As the Americans landed, Sheaffe ordered his Indians and the grenadier company from the 8th Regiment of Foot to meet the invaders on the shoreline. First off the boats was Forsyth, who bellowed, "Men follow me." Lining up his men, he had them fire a volley that decimated the advancing British. The Rifle Regiment then engaged in bitter tree-to-tree firefights until the Indians fled, but the British regulars held their position. Ensign

American and British sailors clash in fierce close quarter fighting.

Joseph Hawley Dwight, 13th US Infantry Regiment, recalled that, "The enemy met us at the water's edge and fought us like men. The militia ran away almost at first fire. The regular [British] troops stood their ground until almost all were killed or wounded."

The US 15th Infantry Regiment landed after the riflemen, with bayonets fixed, under a hail of fire. Pike soon came ashore to assume personal command. His aide-de-camp, Lieutenant Donald Fraser, recalled that as he did, "the balls whistled gloriously" over our heads. As the British grenadiers were pushed back by Forsyth's sharpshooters, Sheaffe arrived with the rest of the 8th Foot, the Newfoundland Fencibles, and a few dozen militia. After falling back before the accurate American shooting, Sheaffe tried but failed to get the Fencibles to renew their advance. As losses mounted, the main body of the British retreated east with the newly arrived Glengarry Light Infantry Regiment covering their withdrawal.

Meanwhile, the American warships duelled with the four British gun batteries, and according to seaman Ned Myers of the USS *Scourge*, the ships were having some "sharp work with the batteries, keeping up a steady fire." At 10:00am, Pike's column moved east along the lake road through a forest. No provision had been made by the British to block the narrow trail the Americans were moving along; instead. the Redcoats remained near the batteries while the Canadian militia milled around Garrison Creek.

By 1:00pm, the Americans had reached Fort York. US artillery commenced to fire at the fortification, while the fleet continued to engage the shore batteries. Suddenly, 300 barrels of gunpowder in the fort's magazine blew up after the retreating British rigged them for demolition, spreading debris over a 500-yard radius. The blast killed dozens of Americans and wounded over 200 others, among them General Pike, who had been observing the action from the Half-Moon Battery. He died later that day. One shocked witness recalled, "The noise of the explosion was tremendous. The earth shook and the sun was darkened. It seemed like heaven and earth were coming together." Meanwhile, Sheaffe evacuated York and marched his men east to Kingston. Colonel Cromwell Pearce, 16th US Infantry Regiment, Pike's successor, failed to press the pursuit of Sheaffe, allowing him to escape.

On April 28, Dearborn accepted York's surrender, and although the one unfinished brig remaining there was destroyed by the British, 20 artillery pieces were captured by the Americans. Over the next two days, the town was sacked by the conquerors. The Parliament Building, Governor's mansion, and military buildings were torched, and many empty homes were robbed. There were no recorded murders or rapes. The fight for York cost the United States Army 60 killed and wounded, with another 38 killed and 222 wounded by the mag-

Death of American Brigadier-General Zebulon Pike at the battle of York (now Toronto) on April 27, 1813. He was killed, alongside 250 US casualties, when the retreating British blew up their gunpowder stocks.

azine explosion. British losses were 59 killed and 94 injured. The American expeditionary force re-embarked on May 1st and sailed for the mouth of the Niagara River, arriving there on the 8th.

✦ ✦ ✦

Following the loss of York, the moment seemed urgent for the British to attack the United States' most important naval asset on Lake Ontario—Sacket's Harbor—since General Vincent's position on the Niagara was in jeopardy, the US squadron under Chauncey was not at Sackets Harbor to defend it, and the military force defending the place was weak. On May 27, Prevost and Yeo gathered from the Kingston area 800 regulars, 60 Fencibles, and a party of Indians—900 men in total and two light cannon, all under Colonel Edward Baynes of the Glengarry Regiment. Eight warships and gunboats, mounting 82 guns and manned by 700 sailors, transported the troops.

The task force sailed from Kingston, only 36 miles from Sackets, and soon the men were ordered into the small boats that would take them ashore. However, rain and strong winds forced them back aboard their transports. Around noon on the 28th, two American schooners detected the approach of the British and sounded the alarm. The Americans spent the day calling in reinforcements to the town and putting them into defensive positions. Relying on the two gun batteries at Fort Tompkins and Fort Volunteer to deter the enemy from entering the harbor, the town's commander, Jacob Brown, placed 600 New York militia and one artillery piece southwest of the village along the water's edge behind an embankment. Behind them were 313 dismounted light dragoons and one gun. On Horse Island, connected to the mainland by a 300 yard causeway, was stationed the 167-strong Albany Volunteers with one gun. Total strength of the American garrison was 1,450 men.

As weak as the American forces were at Sackets Harbor, they were lucky to have a capable leader. Jacob Brown, a Quaker, was born in Pennsylvania on May 9, 1775. Intelligent and brave, Brown was one of the better American generals in the war and his performance at Sackets Harbor would earn him a commission as brigadier general in the US Regular Army.

At 4:30am on the morning of May 29, the British made for a cove a mile from town. From there they were to push up the lakeside wagon road above the cliffs and enter Sackets from the rear. As the British boats neared shore, Lieutenant David Wingfield of the Royal Navy recalled that enemy musket and artillery fire was unleashed on them and that "Almost every shot did execution, which for a moment staggered us." But the British kept approaching, with their gunboats providing covering fire. Prevost brought up the rear of the landing party.

Before reaching the cove, strong winds diverted the landing force to the causeway that connected Horse Shoe Island to the mainland. After gaining the causeway, the British formed and charged across it, routing the American militia to their front. Witnessing the stampede, American Dragoon Lieutenant George Birch recalled that the "militia found the enemy pills too hard to digest and would not wait for a second dose but was making

One of the heroic American moments of the War of 1812 as Perry keeps fighting during the battle of Lake Erie by shifting his command—and his flag—to USS Niagara. Painting by William H. Powell.

the best use of their legs and left the enemy to form and march against us." Behind the militia, the Albany Volunteers loosed a few well-aimed volleys, then retreated back toward the dragoons.

The main body of the attackers started moving northeast along the lakeshore road toward Sackets while the 104th Foot, Canadian Voltigeurs, and Indians pursued the fleeing American militia. The main British column was met by the dragoons who fired disciplined volleys into the Redcoat ranks, but, being outnumbered, could not stop them. The Americans retreated to the town, taking station near a blockhouse and Fort Tompkins. Brown was somewhere to their rear trying to join them when he ran into British troops. He slipped away, spending the rest of the battle rallying his militia.

As the British column neared the west edge of Sackets Harbor, artillery fire from Fort Tompkins, just above the village, showered the troops with cannon balls, supplementing the American musketry already hitting them from the blockhouse sitting on a bluff. Prevost formed his men, not more than 300, and attacked the blockhouse and fort, even though the British ships off to their left were stilled by a lack of wind which prevented them from maneuvering into good firing positions in order to support their army comrades.

The next half hour saw a fierce firefight between the British and the dragoons, with some of the latter drawing away to the east, but a few obstinate American defenders remained to stall the enemy. In the town, Americans burned the stores and equipment at Navy Point shipyard. The British requested that the Americans surrender but the demand was rejected. Staggered by the loss in his command—over half his men were down—and the fleet unable to help, his field artillery not yet come up, and hearing that more American troops were pouring into Sackets from the east, Prevost ordered a withdrawal. The American officers at Fort Tompkins refused to give chase. By 7:30am, the Redcoats were returning to their waiting transports.

The dispirited British sailed for Kingston on May 29, having lost 46 killed and 179 wounded. In return, they captured one artillery piece and 150 prisoners. "The expedition," confessed Prevost in a letter to his government, "has not been attended with the complete success which was expected from it." Tactically a failure, the attack on Sackets Harbor did unnerve Commodore Chauncey enough that he was ever after reluctant to leave it unless

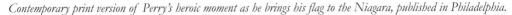

Contemporary print version of Perry's heroic moment as he brings his flag to the Niagara, published in Philadelphia.

it was strongly guarded by land and water. As a result, he based his future plans on protecting his base more than defeating the enemy.

◆ ◆ ◆

"It will not be amongst the least of General Proctor's mortifications," wrote William Henry Harrison to the US Secretary of War, "to find that he has been baffled by a youth who has just passed his twenty-first year." Harrison was reporting on the August 1–2 repulse of the British, under Henry Proctor at Fort Stephenson, located near Sandusky, Ohio by Major George Croghan, 17th US Infantry. This setback, and another failed effort at Fort Meigs in late July, along with dwindling numbers of regular troops and Indians, ended British offensive operations in the west. The next act in that theater would be the decisive battle for Lake Erie.

On July 29, 1813, Richard Barclay inexplicably withdrew his blockading force from Presque Isle, allowing Oliver Perry to bring his ships out of the port into Lake Erie between August 1st and 4th. Perry then conducted sweeps of the lake from a base at Put-in-Bay. Faced with a lack of food and pay, and knowing he would not be receiving any additional manpower for his ships, Barclay weighed anchor from Amherstburg on September 9,

With USS Lawrence *reduced to a wreck by the gunfire of two British ships, Perry was rowed half a mile away under enemy cannon fire to board the* Niagara.

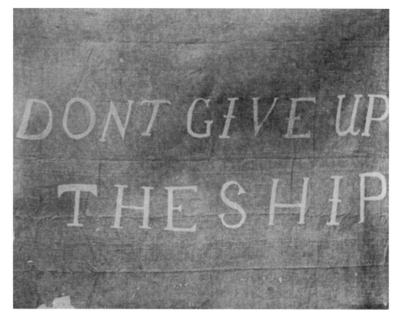

Remains of the flag that Perry first raised on USS Lawrence *during the battle of Lake Erie, displaying the last words of James Lawrence of the USS* Chesapeake *"Don't give up the ship."*

resolving to "sail and risk battle." On Friday the 10th, the opposing squadrons came into contact. The British had three brigs and three schooners, with a total armament of 63 guns; the Americans had two brigs, two schooners, one sloop and four gunboats, mounting 54 cannon.

Barclay hoped to use his longer-ranged weapons to stand off from his more numerous enemy, and pound them from a distance. That tactic could not be employed since the wind proved to be very light, giving the American force the wind advantage, which it used to rapidly close with the British. Perry admonished his captains to "engage your designated adversary, in close action, at half cable's length." He intended to lay alongside the largest British vessels—the 11-gun *Detroit* and 17-gun *Queen Charlotte*—with his most powerful craft, the 20-gun *Lawrence* and 20-gun *Niagara*, while his other ships engaged enemy vessels of equal size. At 10:00am, Perry's ships cleared for action and he raised a dark blue flag displaying the last words of James Lawrence of the USS *Chesapeake*: "Don't give up the ship."

Almost two hours later, Barclay opened fire at 2,000 yards. The two sides closed in line-ahead formation, except for the *Niagara*, which fell behind and did not join the fight until midday. For the next two and a half hours, the *Lawrence* was pummeled by the *Detroit* and *Queen Charlotte*, and reduced to a wreck with 83 of its 103-man crew killed or wounded, and her guns silenced. Perry left the *Lawrence* and rowed half a mile under enemy cannon fire to board the *Niagara*. Jessie Elliott, *Niagara's* skipper, left her to direct the gunboats, while Perry took charge of the ship. On the British side, Barclay, twice wounded, had to relinquish command, while five of six of his ship commanders had been either killed or disabled.

The pivotal moment in the battle occurred when *Queen Charlotte* passed astern of the badly damaged *Detroit* to engage *Niagara* with her starboard battery. The maneuver caused both British ships to become entangled, with *Queen Charlotte's* bowsprit ensnared in *Detroit's* mizzenmast. Unable to move or effectively return the American's fire, which was being delivered at only 100 yards with wood shattering carronades, the two British warships struck their colors at 3.00pm. Soon after, the rest of the British squadron was captured. In this Battle of Lake Erie, the Royal Navy suffered 41 killed, 94 wounded, and 306 captured, compared to an American loss of 27 killed and 96 wounded. With control of Lake Erie, the United States had effectively won the war in the west.

Perry takes the surrender of the British fleet at the battle of Lake Erie aboard the wrecked Lawrence. From painting by W.J. Aylward.

CHAPTER SIX

The Battles of 1813

OPERATIONS IN THE OLD NORTHWEST CAME TO A HEAD IN LATE 1812. AMONG these were the Americans' autumn search-and-destroy missions against the Indians in Ohio and the Indiana and Illinois Territories. They were designed to counter the attacks by Tecumseh that threatened American settlements, as well as Major-General Henry Harrison's left flank as he advanced toward Detroit. To combat this growing menace, punitive expeditions were undertaken.

One such action was led by Lieutenant-Colonel John B. Campbell, 19th United States Infantry Regiment. In mid-December 1812, he set out with 600 cavalry and infantry to destroy the Miami Indian villages along the Mississiniwa River, a tributary of the Wabash, in Indian Territory. On the 18th, his encampment on the Mississiniwa was surprised by a pre-dawn assault by Miami and Pottawatamie braves. According to Private Nathan Vernon, a member of the Pennsylvania volunteer company known as the Pittsburg Blues, the Indian attack was unleashed "as if all the fiends of the lower region had been loosed upon us."

Musket volleys ripped the darkness while the Indians probed for weak spots in the American lines, and the soldiers rushed to shore up any position where the enemy was "playing Hell." At daylight, the Natives drew off and the American cavalry was ordered to pursue, but most did not. One trooper so instructed recorded that "the horse soldiers feared venturing into the Heathen filled timberland and did not obey the order." Unhindered, the enemy made good his escape. US losses were eight killed and 48 wounded; the Indians 47 killed and 75 wounded. With ammunition and food almost gone, and many men suffering from the bitter cold, Campbell started back for Grenville, Ohio, his mission unaccomplished.

"As if all the fiends of the lower region had been loosed upon us"—bitter hand-to-hand fighting as US soldiers clash with Indians during search-and-destroy mission along the Mississiniwa River.

✦ ✦ ✦

Following Harrison's order of late December 1812, James Winchester's column reached the Grand Rapids on the Maumee River on January 10, 1813. By then, Harrison's army had been reduced to 6,300 men. Winchester's own force had fallen by one half to 1,300, due to disease and severe winter weather. According to one of his men, William Atherton, Winchester's soldiers had "nothing but hunger and cold and nakedness staring us in the face." Additionally, his officers and men, mostly Kentuckians, felt that the 60-year-old was militarily incompetent and resented that a Tennessean had been placed over them. Winchester was in fact born in Maryland, but relocated to Tennessee after the Revolutionary War. During that conflict he had been a regular army officer. When he moved out west, he became a general of Tennessee militia and an ardent Republican, factors that explain his appointment in March 1812 as a Brigadier-General in the US Army, and commander of the new Army of the Northwest after Hull was defeated at Detroit. Superseded by Harrison, Winchester supervised the army's left wing, at which point he proved to be a military leader of minimal talent.

Although isolated by 50 miles from the rest of Harrison's army, Winchester was not concerned as he ordered the construction of a poorly located camp on the Maumee River, near today's Perrysburg, Ohio. On the 14th, he dispatched 560 men to capture the hamlet of Frenchtown (modern Monroe, Michigan), 30 miles to the north, which housed 250 Canadian militia and Indians, and a single three-pounder cannon. Reaching his objective on the 18th, Frenchtown, situated on the north bank of the frozen Raisin River, was stormed by the Americans. After taking the village, they chased their enemy into a nearby wood where the pursuers suffered 12 killed and 55 wounded as the Canadians and Indians expertly fell back, firing as they went. After the fight, Winchester moved his entire command to Frenchtown. On January 21, he heard the British were at Brownstown, 18 miles away, preparing to move against him. He dismissed the report as baseless.

At Amherstburg on the 19th, the British Lieutenant-Colonel Henry Proctor addressed his officers, declaring, "My boys, the enemy is upon us and we are going to surprise them"—by attacking Frenchtown. This quick and decisive decision by the normally cautious, methodical professional was out of character, but the right one. Proctor's birthplace was Ireland in 1763. He went from Ensign to Lieutenant-Colonel between 1781 and 1800, mostly by purchase. He was assigned to Canada in 1802, and in mid-1812 was assigned the Western District of Upper Canada by his superior, Brock.

Proctor marched 334 regulars, 212 militia, 28 sailors, and 600 Potawatomi, Miami, and Wyandot Indians, with six small artillery pieces, to Brownstown on the 21st. At dawn the next day the British halted just outside Frenchtown, dressed their lines and positioned their cannons. Alerted by the commotion, the American defenders rushed to the picket fence that passed for a defensive palisade, and commenced shooting at the Redcoats. Caught in the open, the British were cut up badly, forcing them to pull back to a wood. John Richardson, a Canadian volunteer in the 41st Foot Regiment, upon seeing British wounded being killed by American sharpshooters, screamed to his fellow soldiers that "Those wretches are killing our poor defenseless boys." The British artillery, which was intended to clear the Yankees from their position, had 13 of its 16 members mowed down because the guns had been moved too close to the Americans. One of the gunners yelled to his comrades, "Give them canister. They cannot suffer it at this distance." As he loaded his cannon, he was shot dead.

As the British infantry absorbed the withering enemy fire, Proctor's Indian allies poured past both sides of the town and crossed Raisin River. Soon the American line, hit by musket fire from front, flank and rear, broke, as the Kentucky militiamen fled across the water. The Indians, according to one British eyewitness, "with infernal yells followed close on the heels of the fugitives very few of whom received quarter"—finishing them off with tomahawks. Winchester was captured by the Wyandot chief. Not long after, the 385 men of the Kentucky Rifle Regiment in Frenchtown, eager to fight but without ammunition, surrendered on Winchester's order. British losses were 24 regulars and militia killed, with 161 wounded. Indian losses are unknown, while the American loss included 500 prisoners and 400 killed or massacred, 60 of these being wounded men left in Frenchtown and murdered by the Indians.

In the meantime, Harrison had arrived at the Grand Rapids with 900 men. Upon learning of Winchester's debacle at Frenchtown, he withdrew 15 miles to the south. Proctor, his force mauled in the recent contest, heeded his cautious nature and retreated back to Fort Malden. On February 1, 1813, Harrison and 2,000 men returned to the Rapids and constructed Fort Meigs on the south side of the Maumee River as an advanced base, but his effort of the last five months to reach Fort Malden had ground to a halt.

✦   ✦   ✦

In early 1813, US President James Madison selected John Armstrong, a US Army Brigadier-General and commander of the defenses of New York City, and member of an anti-Madison faction of the Republican Party, as the new Secretary of War. Born on November 25, 1758 in Carlisle, Pennsylvania, he joined the Continental Army in 1775, serving at the battles of Trenton, Princeton and Saratoga. Mustered out of the army as a major, Armstrong showed a canny knack for intrigue. Moving to New York, he joined the Republican Party, supported Thomas Jefferson for President, and served as US Senator from the Empire State, as well as American Ambassador to France. As the chief administrator of the War Department, he sought to be the nation's primary military strategist by personally directing the movements of the principal armies. He also harbored presidential ambitions.

Along with a new Secretary of War came an effort to increase the size of the Amer-

Re-enactors recreate 6th US Infantry Regiment at drill.

*Re-enactor holds
Brown Bess musket.
He recreates a British
private of the 8th
(King's) Regiment
of Foot.*

ican army. During the first months of 1813, Congress authorized the creation of six new
major-generals, eight additional brigadier-generals, and an increase in the strength of the
army from 35,752 to 57,351.

"Harrison's army is for all purposes dissolved," wrote an officer on the General's
staff in late February 1813, because, as he complained, "his Ohio and Kentucky militia
finished their six months service and have happily returned home." The War Department's
new campaign blueprint for Harrison was based on control of Lake Erie. Once this was
accomplished, he would transport his force by water, assuring the capture of Detroit and
Malden, as well as securing the frontier. The administration decreed he could have no more
than 7,000 men, since his British opposition in the area numbered no more than 2,000,
and because the United States Treasury could not afford to maintain a larger force in the
west.

Harrison's opponent, Henry Proctor—recently promoted to Brigadier—understood
the dual threat the Americans posed to Fort Malden: Fort Meigs as a base for a land or sea
assault, and Presque Isle where construction of enemy ships menaced British control of
Lake Erie and thus Upper Canada. While the garrison at Meigs was weak—just 500 men

Battle of Fort Stephenson, August 2, 1813, in which the British aided by Indians led by Tecumseh attacked the fort on the Sandusky River but were repulsed.

through March—and Presque Isle was defenseless, Proctor did not strike by using his control of the lake to concentrate his forces for an assault on either American position. The more important target was the US naval base, which if taken would have assured British dominance of Lake Erie, and thus the safety of Fort Malden. But Proctor remained inactive, pleading he could undertake no offensive moves due to lack of supplies, transport and poor weather. He blamed his superior, the new British commander of Upper Canada, Major-General Francis de Rottenburg, for the first two impediments.

De Rottenburg came from Poland, and gained his first military experiences in the French Army, but he moved on to the British Army and was promoted Major-General in 1810. In Canada, he exhibited proven combat leadership as well as administrative skill, and succeeded Isaac Brock as head of Upper Canada in June 1813. His first inclination after taking over responsibility was to abandon the province. He did not do so, but that initial mindset may have been the reason he failed to provide Proctor with the means to tackle Fort Meigs or Presque Isle. His performance in 1813 showed him as "the solid but undistinguished Baron [who] exhibited few signs of brilliance, originality or forceful determination."

Proctor's reluctance to move ended on April 24, when he left Fort Malden with 984 regulars and militia, sailed down the Maumee, was joined by Tecumseh and 1,200 Indians, and landed below Fort Meigs. On May 1, his seven heavy guns commenced bombarding the American fortification, constructed of earth and heavy logs on a bluff 60 feet above the Maumee. Surrounded by the river on its north, to the east and west by deep ravines, and on its southern face by a log palisade, its garrison numbered 1,100 men and 30 cannon.

For seven days, the British bombarded the American position that had been strengthened by a traverse—a high protective wall of earth the length of the camp. According to Proctor's report, the traverse was so effective "as to render unavailing every effort of our Artillery." Frustrated by the strong defenses, Tecumseh dared Harrison to come out and give battle, and not hide "behind logs and in the earth like a groundhog." Harrison wisely refused, expecting a relief column of 1,200 Kentucky militiamen under Brigadier-General Green Clay any moment. With them, he planned a counterattack, taking 800 of Clay's men down the Maumee and attacking the British batteries on the north bank, while other Kentucky militia came ashore on the south side. After both groups were established on land, Harrison would lead a sortie from the fort to join them.

On May 5, the American force landed on the north shore and took the enemy guns, but before spiking them set about chasing the Indians in the area. Proctor hit back, recovered his artillery, and after a vicious fight killed 200 of Clay's men and captured 500 more. Proctor lost 50 men, not including Indians. Meanwhile, the American party that was to land on the south side of the river was prevented from doing so by the strong current, making their way instead to Fort Meigs. A third contingent tried to land on the north bank to help their beleaguered comrades, but was forced to escape to the fort. Harrison, witnessing the plight of this last group of Americans, sent out 350 men from Meigs to take an enemy battery on the south side of the river. This unit, under Colonel John Miller, succeeded in reaching and spiking the guns but had to retreat when attacked by an overwhelming number of Indians. As at Frenchtown, after the battle Americans captured on the north bank were murdered by the Indians until Tecumseh halted the massacre.

On May 9, Proctor gave up his siege and returned to Fort Malden. His Indians were leaving him, the Canadian militia clamored to be released to go home to put in their crops, and many others were down with sickness. A pause now settled over major operations in the Northwest. Harrison was ordered to assume the defensive until Lake Erie was in American hands and his army's ranks were filled. Proctor, soon promoted to Major-General, did not stir because little by way of additional men and material reached him due to pressure exerted on the British along the Niagara front.

✦ ✦ ✦

On the Niagara front, Major-General Henry Dearborn set up camp at Four Mile Creek with 4,700 American troops poised to strike the British bastion of Fort George four miles to the east. Dearborn's new chief-of-staff was Colonel Winfield Scott. Born in Virginia on June 13, 1786, Scott was an attorney before entering the US Army in 1808 as a Captain, rising to Lieutenant- Colonel in 1812. Captured at the battle of Queenston, he was exchanged in March 1813 and promoted Colonel. His natural leadership abilities, combined with great physical bravery, indomitable will and aggressiveness made him the driving force behind the timid, unimaginative Dearborn.

Scott's plan for the capture of Fort George called for transporting troops from Four

Fort George, Lake Ontario, captured by the Americans from the British on May 27, 1813. Now a preserved national site.

Naval cannon mounted on section of reconstructed battlements at Fort George.

Mile Creek along the shore of Lake Ontario and landing them behind the fort. Close coordination between the army and the supporting naval force was required. Scott would command the lead elements of the attackers. Defending the area around Fort George with 1,800 British regulars, 500 militia, and 100 Indians was Brigadier-General John Vincent. Modest and well liked, the Irish-born Vincent was a capable, if not exceptional, military leader.

At 3:00am on May 27, American troops shoved off in boats on Lake Ontario while warships silenced the two British batteries defending the landing beach. Oliver Hazard Perry directed the naval gunfire and the movement of the soldiers to shore. Vincent had determined to meet the American assault on the beach and placed almost his entire command there. Colonel George McFeely, 22nd US Infantry Regiment, was in the first assault wave and remembered that, as his men pulled for the coastline, the enemy "lay in waiting in a ravine 40 yards from the shore. They reserved their fire until our boats were within 150 yards when they opened a heavy and galling fire." He reported that, upon reaching the shore, "the action was very close and warm for about ten minutes after we landed, when the [British] army gave way and retreated in confusion." As the Americans hit the beach, the US Navy, according to a sailor called Myers, "kept up a steady fire with grape and canister, until the boats [small landing craft] got in shore, and were engaged with the enemy, when we threw round-shot over the heads of our men, upon the English."

Other accounts of the initial American landings paint a picture of a hard fight to secure the beachhead. As the American advance guard, led by Scott and Perry, set foot on land, they were met by British defenders atop a 12-foot embankment who pushed them back with a bayonet charge. Scott held his nerve and led a successful countercharge that drove the enemy from the high ground. Outnumbered by the American troops coming ashore and suffering from the supporting fire of several US Navy schooners, the British, after two valiant but fruitless counterattacks, broke and left the field. Soon after, Vincent ordered the abandonment of Fort George, Chippawa and Fort Erie, and moved his command 18 miles beyond Queenston to his supply depot at Beaver Dams.

Having secured Fort George, Scott continued in pursuit of Vincent until told to terminate the chase, for fear of ambush, and return to the fort. The capture of Fort George cost the Americans 40 killed and 113 wounded, compared to a British loss of 108 killed, 163 wounded, and 115 prisoners—all regulars—as well as most of the militia captured. The British abandonment of Fort Erie freed the American naval force at Black Rock, allowing US ships safe passage to Presque Isle. However, the true objective of the operation, the elimination of Vincent's command, was not obtained and would remain a serious thorn in the Americans' side.

Had the Americans been firmer in their pursuit of Vincent after Fort George, claimed Lieutenant-Colonel John Harvey, the British army would have been "caught under a circumstance of every possible disadvantage." One of the best British officers in North America, Harvey, General Vincent's second-in-command, was in a position to know. Destruction of Vincent's Niagara army would have left Proctor in the west isolated, and all Upper Canada exposed to American aggression. Instead, the army under Vincent would live to fight another day.

On June 1, 1813, General Dearborn decided to complete the unfinished business of eliminating Vincent's army, which had withdrawn to Burlington Heights at the western tip of Lake Ontario. He sent out 1,400 men, under Brigadier-General William Henry Winder, from Maryland to finish Vincent off. Although a Federalist, Winder was appointed Lieutenant-Colonel in the Regular Army in 1812, even though he had no military experience. After arriving near Vincent's fortified location, Winder realized that he was outnumbered and requested reinforcements.

Dearborn sent out Brigadier-General John Chandler, a Revolutionary War veteran with very limited military experience, who was a militia officer before the war. He assumed command of the expedition that had a combined force of 3,030 infantry, artillery, and cavalry. Upon studying the British position on Burlington Heights, Chandler decided not to make a frontal assault but to march from Stoney Creek to the lake, cross Burlington beach and cut Vincent's route to York.

On June 5, the Americans fought a sharp skirmish with an enemy picket formed by the Light Company of the 49th Foot, near Big Creek, forcing them to withdraw to a camp at Stoney Creek, 10 miles from Burlington Heights. The site was a good one with a 20-

Line of British redcoat re-enactors advance against Americans in skirmish at Fort George.

Scots troops come under fire as they cross the frozen river at Ogdensburg in February 1813.

foot-high ridgeline to its front overlooking a grassland meadow; the American left rested on the high ground, the right was by a swamp. The troops were arranged with 800 men placed three miles from the main camp, the remainder in the encampment. The troops posted that night were as follows: the 25th US Infantry Regiment and the light troops on the right, the 23rd, 16th, and 5th US Infantry on the left. The artillery was placed in the center, but without support. Four hundred yards behind the artillery, Burn's Light Dragoons were camped. Surrounding the camp were scores of advanced pickets.

Responding to the American presence, Vincent approved Colonel Harvey's plan for a night attack with 766 men, with Harvey leading the assault. At 2:30am on June 6 the British attacked, guided to their objectives by American campfires. As the British approached, some of their staff officers started to cheer in violation of Harvey's "perfect order and profound silence command." British Lieutenant James Fitzgibbon, 49th Foot, heard the shouting and recalled, "The instant I heard their shout I considered our affair ruined."

The alerted Americans sprang up and commenced firing at their attackers. The Redcoats returned the fire against orders—the plan of attack being a swift advance with the bayonet. However, many of the American units were still surprised by the onslaught, one officer of the 2nd US Artillery Regiment recording that, "The enemy, with Indians, surprised with horrid yelling, and attacked our advanced guard, which we composed. We were able to make but a feeble resistance as the enemy was not more than 15 yards from us and obliged us to retire in great confusion."

Upon hearing the noise of battle, Chandler took command in the center of the American line, while Winder took over the left. Hearing firing from the right, Chandler galloped in that direction but was badly injured when his horse threw him. Limping back to the center of the line, he arrived to find his artillery had been captured by the British, and he was soon taken by the enemy as well.

At the start of the battle the British had made little headway as they exchanged fire with the more numerous US troops. The Americans, Harvey recalled, "poured a destructive fire of musketry upon us, which we answered on our part by repeated charges whenever a body of the enemy would be discerned or reached." American Colonel James Burn said that during the one-sided firefight, "the enemy attempted by frequent charges to break our line, but without effect, being obliged to give way by the well-directed fire of our brave troops." Entire British companies, torn by American musketry, began to retreat just half an hour after their initial assault. At this point, soldiers from the 49th Foot, under Major Charles Plenderleath, charged the center of the American line to silence the artillery that was taking its toll on the attackers. The Major lost his horse and was wounded twice, but his action retrieved British fortunes from the edge of disaster. These were the soldiers who took Chandler captive. Not long after Chandler was taken, Winder rode to the American center and was also taken prisoner.

Although the official reports on the Battle of Stoney Creek differed—the Americans saying they repulsed the British, while the British claimed that the Americans were routed—it appears that both sides were in retreat at the climax of the fight, and that the British thrust at the US artillery gave them time to take away two artillery pieces and some prisoners. With their generals captured, command of the American army devolved on Colonel Burn, 2nd US Light Dragoons. He withdrew his force a mile from the battlefield to reorganize, admitting in a private letter that he was "at a loss on that occasion" as to what to do. Burn then ordered a withdrawal to Forty Mile Creek, since the army was nearly out of ammunition, and completely out of generals.

Both sides rallied by dawn, so both claimed victory even though the battle was a draw. The British commander, Vincent, had played little part in the drama since early on he was thrown from his horse, disoriented by the fall, and spent most of the day wandering in a wood several miles from the battlefield. He was discovered by his men later that day. The British marched to Stoney Creek after their demoralized, leaderless opponents vacated the spot. American losses were 17 killed, 38 wounded and 113 captured. The British lost 23 killed, 136 wounded and 55 missing.

✦ ✦ ✦

In the second week of June, Royal Navy Captain James Yeo had gone to aid Vincent in the western part of Lake Ontario. Instead of following him, the American Commodore Issac Chauncey stayed snugly in Sackets Harbor, thus giving the British control of the lake by default. Vincent took the opportunity the American naval leader provided him by advancing from Stoney Creek east to Beaver Dams. Responding, Dearborn pulled his forces back toward Fort George, relinquishing almost all the territory the Americans held west of the Niagara River, including Fort Erie. On December 10, Fort George was abandoned by the Americans, followed on the 18th by a daring British night attack that captured Fort Niagara, on the US side of the Niagara River, and its 400-man American garrison.

With Dearborn again ill and Chandler and Winder in British captivity, Brigadier-General John Parker Boyd became *de facto* regional commander. Desiring to gain elbowroom and raise the spirits of the troops, Boyd dispatched a force to attack an enemy post at De Cou's House, 12 miles from American lines. Boyd had served for 20 years as a mercenary for feuding princes in India after leaving the United States army in 1789. In 1808, he rejoined the army as a colonel, and fought well at the battles of Tippecanoe and at Fort George under Dearborn. He was made Brigadier-General in the regular army in 1812.

Indian allies of the British attack Fort Dearborn (on the site of Chicago), August 15, 1813.

The force sent on the De Cou's House mission involved 575 men, including infantry, cavalry, and two artillery pieces under Lieutenant-Colonel Charles Boerstler, setting off on the night of June 23. His march put him beyond any supporting friendly units. That night, too, a woman named Laura Secord, the wife of a Canadian militia officer, had learned of the Americans' plans had gone to warn the British. The next day, upon reaching Beaver Dams, the Americans were ambushed by 465 Indians and surrounded. The fight had been going on for three hours when a detachment of British regulars under Lieutenant Fitzgibbon appeared and demanded the Americans surrender, threatening a massacre by the Indians if they continued to resist. Boerstler threw in the towel and he and his men became prisoners of war. Fitzgibbon later reported that: "Not a shot was fired on our side by any but the Indians. They beat the American detachment into a state of terror."

The fight at Beaver Dams brought Dearborn's Niagara Campaign to an inglorious end. It also gave Secretary of War Armstrong the excuse to relieve Dearborn from command, replacing him temporarily with Boyd. No further reverses came to American arms in the summer of 1813 since the new British commander of Upper Canada—Major-General de Rottenburg—was as lacking in enterprise as his American counterparts.

✦   ✦   ✦

"The loss of the fleet is a most calamitous circumstance," wrote British Brigadier-General Proctor. "I do not see the least chance of occupying to advantage my present extensive position." American control of Lake Erie completely isolated the British in Western Upper Canada from supplies and manpower coming from the east. Proctor's 900 regulars and 1,100 Indians were no match for Harrison's reported 6,000 troops. Proctor abandoned Amherstburg and Fort Malden on September 24 and took up the 70-mile march to the lower Thames River Valley as a preliminary move further east to join Vincent. Outraged with what they considered the British Crown's abandonment of their cause, Tecumseh and many of the Indians only reluctantly joined the British retreat.

After occupying Fort Malden on the 27th, the American pursuit of their enemy did not commence immediately. Harrison wanted to lead off the chase with Colonel Richard M. Johnson's 500-man well-trained and equipped Kentucky Mounted Rifle Regiment, which did not reach him until October 1. Next day the American army, 3,500 strong, moved out. By the 3rd, Johnson, supported by Perry's gunboats, was nipping at Proctor's heels despite the week's head start the British had on their pursuers. On October 5, the British and their Indian allies, including the women and children that had accompanied their supply train, took up a defensive position on the north bank of the Thames, two miles west of the village of Moraviantown. Proctor placed the 41st Foot, formed in two lines in open order formation—one behind the other 200 yards apart—on his left in a wood next to the Thames. To Ensign James Cochran of the 41st Foot, the British formation was not a reliable one, noting that "the order of the lines was neither extended nor close but somewhat irregularly between both, and the trees were not sufficiently large to afford protection." The Indians were posted on the right on the edge of a swamp. One six-pounder cannon

American cavalry clash with British-allied Indians at the battle of the Thames, October 5, 1813.

was planted on the road in front of the 41st. Proctor's force numbered 430 regulars and 600 braves.

Harrison planned to send his regulars, under Lewis Cass, against the 41st while his militia masked the Indian position. Johnson was to be held in reserve. But Johnson, the amateur soldier and sitting US Congressman from Kentucky, proposed that he be allowed to initiate a mounted charge on the spread-out Redcoats of the 41st. After receiving Harrison's bemused approval, Johnson sent his battalions straight at the British. Shouting "Remember the River Raisin!" the black-clad riders charged, were halted by enemy fire, but charged again, breaking through both British lines, then wheeled right and left to bring rifle fire on the Redcoats from the rear. Upon contact with the onrushing horsemen, according to Private Shadrach Byfield of the 41st Foot, "After exchanging a few shots our men gave way." The lone British artillery piece never got off a shot, since it was dragged into the wood by its startled team. In five minutes, at a cost of three wounded Americans, the fight ended with the British surrendering.

Turning now to the Indians, Johnson spurred his horsemen into the swamp and was received by a deadly musket volley, which dropped most of the Kentucky vanguard and wounded Johnson. The area was too thick for effective mounted action, so Johnson ordered his men to dismount, and a furious firefight, along with many hand-to-hand combats, ensued. Tecumseh was in the act of rallying his warriors when he was killed by a musket ball. Upon his death, recalled Kentucky Private William Greathouse, the Indians "gave the loudest yells I ever heard from human beings and that ended the fight." Reinforced by more American regiments, and with some of Johnson's men gaining their rear, the Indians broke and fled through the forest.

The Battle of the Thames was concluded in less than an hour. American losses were 12 killed and 22 wounded; the British lost 12 killed, 22 wounded, and 579 captured; the Indians 33 killed, including Tecumseh. Proctor and 246 soldiers, and the accompanying women and children, escaped to Burlington Heights, reaching there on the 17th. Fearing a further advance by the Americans, Prevost ordered the evacuation of Upper Canada up to Kingston. But Harrison, instead of continuing on, returned to Detroit. He did so because his militia's term of service was about to expire and he would not have the men to follow Proctor. It was also obvious that the British and Indians would no longer be a threat to the Northwest. By mid-October most of the latter had entered into an armistice with the United States. The fighting in the west was over. Attention now turned to the east.

✦   ✦   ✦

Upon learning that Dearborn had been replaced by Major-General James Wilkinson, an army wag quipped that "age and fatuity were being replaced by age and imbecility." James Wilkinson—a confidence man in uniform, as well as being a paid agent of Spain—was born in Maryland on January 1, 1757. Present with Benedict Arnold during his Quebec Expedition, then a captain in the Continental Army, he was made brevet Brigadier-General in 1777 after working on Horatio Gates' staff. Charges of financial corruption caused him to leave the Army in 1781, whereupon he moved to Kentucky, then New Orleans, where he worked as a spy for the Spanish in return for being allowed by them a trade monopoly. Returning to the US Army in 1792, he was appointed Lieutenant-Colonel, then Brigadier-General in 1796—the most senior army officer in the country. As governor of the Missouri Territory he renewed his ties as a Spanish agent and plotted to create a breakaway state allied to Spain in the southwest. As head of the Seventh Military District at New Orleans, he occupied Mobile for the United States in April 1813. In July of that year he was promoted Major-General and tasked with conducting a campaign against Montreal.

The offensive was planned by Armstrong who envisioned a two-thrust operation: Wilkinson moving from Sackets Harbor in a flotilla of small craft that would transit the St. Lawrence River, while a second column marched up the Champlain River Valley into Lower Canada to rendezvous with him. The forces would then unite for the drive on Montreal, which along with Quebec, was the most important British supply and staging area in North America. The commander of the second prong of the offensive was Major-General Wade Hampton, whose hatred of Wilkinson only made the already quixotic attempt on Montreal more misguided.

Raised in South Carolina, Hampton had fought as a partisan during the Revolutionary War, distinguishing himself at the battle of Eutaw Springs. After that conflict, he amassed a huge fortune selling cotton. He won a seat in the US House of Representatives, and was then made Colonel of the Regiment of Light Dragoons. In 1809, he became a Brigadier-General and succeeded Wilkinson as commander in New Orleans, where he and

Winfield Scott gained his predecessor's enmity by exposing the poor administration of his command. In March 1813 he was promoted to Major-General and was transferred from Norfolk, Virginia to Burlington, New York in preparation for an eventual attack on Lower Canada. Flatly refusing to obey orders from Wilkinson who was his senior, Hampton was talked into cooperating with him only by being promised that his orders would come through Secretary of War Armstrong.

The operation was held in abeyance until the American troops under General Boyd at Fort George could be ferried to Sackets Harbor. That was made possible after a daylong sparring match between the ships of Chauncey and Yeo's squadrons on September 28 near Burlington Bay, which resulted in the British retreat to Kingston, thus giving temporary control of Lake Ontario to the United States. Although Armstrong wanted to first take Kingston before heading for Montreal, he changed his mind upon learning on October 16 that the former had been heavily reinforced. By that same date, according to his later writings, he felt Montreal could not be taken so late in the season, and gave instructions for the preparation of winter quarters for his troops of the Northern Army, a clear admission that the invasion of Canada was being suspended. But political pressure was growing for the American Army to go on the offensive, and Armstrong and Wilkinson bent to that pressure. The invasion, which should have been shelved, was on again even though winter was near.

Wilkinson's 8,000-man army left Sackets Harbor piecemeal, starting up the St. Lawrence on October 16, with the whole to concentrate at French Creek—modern Clayton, New York. Meanwhile, Hampton had crossed into Lower Canada on September 19. Looking for water for his men, he marched his 4,000 raw recruits 40 miles west to the Chateauguay River. Waiting there for him, only 35 miles from Montreal, was Lieutenant-Colonel Charles-Michel de Salaberry, a native of Quebec. The Colonel had joined the British Army in 1792, fought in the West Indies, Ireland and Holland, and was sent to Canada in 1810.

Taking station with his force of 1,800 regulars and militia, where the 100-foot-wide, six-foot-deep water course made a sharp bend, de Salaberry set up a two-mile-deep defense with a number of wooden breastworks to the rear of an abatis—his left was shielded by the river, his right by a marsh. Across the right bank of the river, he placed 160 men to guard a ford located two miles behind his forward defense lines.

Upon Hampton's approach to the Chateauguay on October 25, he detached 2,000 men under Colonel Robert Purdy to cross the river and head for the ford behind the enemy. This force advanced only five miles before becoming disoriented, ending up not behind the Canadians but along the river opposite de Salaberry's first defensive line. During mid-morning on the 26th, the Americans of Brigadier-General George Izard's 2nd Brigade took position opposite the abates. Izard made a demonstration with his 10th US Infantry Regiment, slowly reinforcing his line with other units. Reacting to this move, de Salaberry moved men to the first defensive position, stationing himself there as well. He then ordered his bugler to "sound for commence firing and a brisk little action took place."

At 11:00am, Purdy's 1st Brigade marched for the ford, his advance elements running into a British militia company on the right side of the river. A 20-minute firefight broke out, and according to Sergeant Neff, US 4th Infantry, it was a "furious action supported with firmness on both sides when we charged the enemy and drove him off." Actually, both parties were shaken and retreated. Hampton soon cancelled his plan to take the ford, recalled the 1st Brigade, and ordered it to pull back a few miles and re-cross to the left bank of the river.

At 2:00pm, Izard was directed to attack the enemy abatis. The general formed his three regiments in line and let loose a series of volleys. Corporal Bishop, 29th US Infantry Regiment, remembered that his unit "first halted under the brow of a hill and was ordered to load our muskets at which time the battle commenced at a very hot note." Returning fire in front of the abatis were the Canadian Fencibles, whose aim was good, with many American wounded being hit in the head or chest. The exchange of fire then slackened as both sides turned their attention to the other side of the river.

On the right bank, as Purdy recorded, "The enemy made a furious attack on the column by a great discharge of musketry, accompanied by the yells of savages." The order to retreat was then heard, and the 1st Brigade, abandoned by many of its officers who had left the battle previously, recoiled. Some rallied and these fended off a charge by the Canadians, pursuing them to the Chateauguay where the Americans were fired on by Canadian Voltigeurs across the river. This "checked their career," said one soldier, "and threw them back in the greatest confusion." After that, Purdy's outfit was out of the fight.

At 3:00pm, Hampton ordered Izard to disengage his men and retreat three miles to their camp. He failed to inform Purdy of this move, leaving the 1st Brigade isolated on the other side of the river until it crossed and joined Hampton next day. De Salaberry and his victorious command remained in their position for the next eight days just in case the Americans returned. The Canadian casualties at the battle of Chateauguay numbered five killed, 15 wounded, and four missing; the Americans lost 50 officers and enlisted men.

After this humiliation, Hampton withdrew from Canada to Plattsburg, New York and entered winter quarters. Soon thereafter, he refused to obey an order from Wilkinson to move his army to Canada and join him. He then tendered his resignation and left the army. As Hampton marched out of Canada, Wilkinson and his army, escorted by 12 gunboats and 300 small craft, marched in. Not until November 6 did the expedition, lashed by gales and snowstorms, approach Prescott, 60 miles from their starting point at Sackets Harbor.

On October 17, de Rottenburg got wind of Wilkinson's move, and dispatched Lieutenant Colonel Joseph W. Morrison, 89th Foot Regiment, with 630 men and two light artillery pieces on several schooners and gunboats, to act as a corps of observation to dog the American force. Next day, augmented by men and additional cannon, Morrison landed his 1,200 troops at Prescott, behind the Americans. The escorting gunboats, under Captain William Howe Mulcaster, Royal Navy, continued to shadow the enemy and harass the American craft on the St. Lawrence.

Positioned at the John Chrysler farm, Morrison took up a position in case the Americans decided to turn on him. Just to his rear was a dirt road which aided lateral movement along his line; a log fence lining it provided good cover. To his left was an impassable swampy pinewood a half-mile inland. To the front of the British were a ploughed field, two gullies, and a large ravine that bent down to the river. Morrison placed the bulk of the 89th and 49th Regiments north to south along the dirt track. Captain George W. Barnes' three companies of the 89th, two companies of the 49th, and two of the Canadian Fencibles under Thomas Pearson were placed behind the first gully; Fraser's dragoons at the ravine; Frederick Heriot's light troops above the ravine in the woods; and two guns on the right of the main line, and one with Pearson. Thirty Mohawk Indians were in the woods on the extreme British left.

On the 11th, a gray Thursday, the American army was on the north shore of the river while their boats navigated the Longue Salte Rapids. Serving as the rearguard was Boyd's division, three brigades and 3,000 men strong, with orders that "should the enemy harass the rear," Boyd was to "turn and beat him back." At 2:00pm, Brigadier Robert Swartout's 4th Brigade, Boyd's Division, came to the aid of American pickets being pressured by Heriot's light troops and the Mohawks. He was followed by Brigadier-General Leonard Covington's 3rd Brigade, with Colonel Isaac Coles's Brigade moving on his right. The men of the 3rd and 4th Brigades became disorganized due to the rough terrain and effective skirmishing from Heriot's men, but forced the British back. As the three American units cleared the woods, they found themselves in front of the main British line across a large open field.

Seeing the Americans leave the woods, the 49th and 89th moved forward and deployed in a line of two ranks. The approaching Americans were an imposing sight, with one Sergeant of the 49th exclaiming that "there are too many, we shall be slaughtered!" As the Americans came on, they were hit by a "heavy and galling fire" from the British artillery on the field and from Royal Navy gunboats.

The American infantry tried to form and return fire but were unable to properly do so. One US officer remarked that "we could not recover any order." Coles's men, marching between the other brigades, became so disordered that according to Lieutenant Joseph Dwight, 30th US Infantry, the men "retreated in great disorder" under the artillery fire. Only with difficulty were the Americans rallied.

Boyd ordered Swartout and Coles to attack the British left flank. The former advanced and then began to deploy into line but became disorganized. The left flank companies of the 89th swung 90 degrees back and delivered a lethal volley at the struggling Americans, which staggered Swartout's front ranks. The shattered formation retreated, colliding with Coles's Brigade and sending the lot to the rear in panic.

Meanwhile, Covington's 3rd Brigade steered for the ravine and forced that position. Morrison, seeing the threat to his right, sent his main line to confront the US 3rd Brigade. The opposing lines closed to within 100 yards, with the Yankees firing "irregular, a pop, pop, popping all the time," according to a British officer, while the Redcoat volleys were

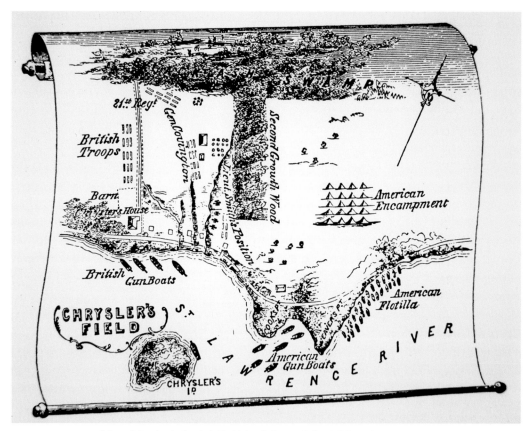

Map of battle of Crysler's Field (spelled wrongly here), November 11, 1813.

"all together and at regular intervals like tremendous rolls of thunder." The exchange lasted 15 minutes before the American ranks were thinned and their ammunition exhausted. According to Colonel Cromwell Pearce, 16th US Infantry, they "deemed it proper [for the division] to return to the ravine." The Americans—the three brigades mixed up—gained the ravine, and a stalemate between the opposing infantry ensued.

At 3:30pm, some relief was afforded the Americans by the arrival of four six-pounders, which began shooting at the 49th Foot. Tormented by the enemy fire, the 49th attacked the guns but were thrown back with loss. Morrison mentioned the attempt on the American artillery when he wrote that the 49th was "directed to charge the guns posted opposite to ours, but it became necessary within a short distance to check the forward movement in consequence of a new threat." John Sewell, an officer in the 49th, identified the threat when he observed American cavalry "galloping up the high road" directly at the 49th's right flank.

The 2nd Light Dragoon Regiment, under Major John T. Woodford, was propelled forward in order to save the US artillery now being threatened by a renewed British attack, this time by parts of the 89th Foot. Thundering onward, they were struck by canister from

British artillery, as well as musket balls from Barnes' soldiers. Shaken, the blue-clad horsemen continued on and were almost upon the 49th's right flank, when the latter swung back, and, as stated by Lieutenant Sewell, "poured in [a] volley" at them at the same time as Barnes fired into their rear. The dragoon's formation fell apart, those not shot from their saddles running for the ravine. Woodford continued to ride forward, and again according to Sewell, "leapt over the fence and was riding toward our right, but alone; some of the men rushed out to attack him with their bayonets fixed, but observing that he was unassisted he took the fence again in good hunting style and followed his men who were in good retreat." The American riders lost 18 killed and 12 wounded. However, the charge had not been in vain as it allowed three of the four American guns to escape capture.

With the enemy cavalry gone, Morrison moved his entire force west of the ravine to continue the contest. Boyd was of another mind. Feeling he had executed his orders from Wilkinson to drive away any probing enemy, he related, "I ordered the main body to fall back, and reform where the action first commenced"—in other words, at the edge of the woods. His three brigades duly turned and marched to the forest. With a fresh supply of musket balls on hand, men and officers expected to renew the battle, but it was not to be. Boyd received an order to fall back to the American boats where the army would be moved two miles downriver and landed on the US side. His division formed a column of march and proceeded as instructed. After two hours and 20 minutes, the battle of Chrysler's Farm, the most critical battle fought during the War of 1812, was over. Montreal was never again seriously threatened. British battle losses totaled 22 killed, 148 wounded and nine missing; the American army had 102 killed, including General Covington, and 237 wounded.

Wilkinson received a letter from Hampden on the 12th that gave him the excuse to terminate the operation. Hampden's missive explained that since Armstrong did not think taking Montreal was feasible, therefore Hampton was not going to join Wilkinson in Canada. Wilkinson's army wintered at French Mills on the Salmon River. Most of the British force opposing him returned to either Prescott or Kingston. Thus the year ended with America's gains on the Niagara forfeit, the St. Lawrence Campaign a failure, and its total war effort at its nadir.

Fifteen minutes of gunfire between the Chesapeake *and* Shannon *culminated in a bloody hand-to-hand fight.*

CHAPTER SEVEN

Warships and Privateers

⤳⟨⟨⟨⟨⟩⟩⟩⟩⤶

THE WAR "SEEMS TO ASSUME A NEW AS WELL AS MORE ACTIVE AND INVETERATE aspect than before," wrote Admiral Warren to the British Admiralty on October 5, 1812. His assessment was correct—the Madison administration was adamant in prosecuting the war as long as Britain refused to renounce impressments, and Yankee privateers were menacing British maritime trade from the West Indies to the St. Lawrence River. Just as enraging was the fact that the upstart American Navy had won two single-ship actions. To rectify this unexpected situation, His Majesty's Royal Navy installed a new chief of the North Atlantic Station with authority over the entire United States coastline from Maine to Louisiana, all the inland lakes, and the West Indies.

John Borlase Warren had been in the Royal Navy since 1771, starting as an able seaman. From an aristocratic family, he had been a Member of Parliament, and in 1810 was made Admiral after almost 40 years serving at every command level in the navy dating back to the American Revolution. Two years later, the 59 year-old—known more his for diplomatic and administrative capabilities than his combat skills—was placed in charge of the naval effort against the United States.

By 1813 Warren had instituted a multi-faceted program to combat American naval activities. They included sealing enemy warships and privateers in port, assuring British naval dominance on the Great Lakes and Lake Champlain, and creating a blockade of all principal ports south of Rhode Island, including the Mississippi, to put "a complete stop to all trade and intercourse by sea and with these ports." At first, New England was treated differently. The British government wanted all US naval operations from those anchorages halted, but not commercial traffic. To that end, New England separatism was to be encouraged by the generous issuance of trading licenses allowing them to carry on commerce with Britain.

Safeguarding Britain's trade traffic in his area of authority was also the Admiral's responsibility. This included providing escorts for ship convoys when needed. Lastly, he was tasked with pinning down enemy ground forces along the coast through amphibious raids, so they could not be used against Canada. For this purpose, in 1813, two Royal Marine battalions were transferred from Spain and Holland—a total of 1,600 men—to work directly with the British fleet in American waters.

To accomplish the blockade of the American East Coast, Warren commanded, early in 1813, 97 warships ranging from ships-of-the-line to frigates to brigs and sloops. However, the size of the British contingent could do little against adverse weather and prevailing tide conditions, especially during the winter months of November to March, when contrary winds blew ships off their stations, and the same winds, accompanied by thick fog, enabled American warships and commerce marauders to escape port.

As Warren scrapped together an effective naval force to blockade the United States and control the inland lakes, American naval action was taking a new turn. In December 1812, Paul Hamilton was replaced by 52-year-old William Jones as Navy Secretary. Pennsylvania-born, he served in the Continental Army at the battles of Trenton and Princeton, and was later a lieutenant in the Continental Navy. During the inter-war years he was involved in the mercantile trade. As a Republican, President Jefferson offered him the position of Secretary of the Navy in 1801, but Jones declined. On January 12, 1813, he accepted the job from President Madison.

Jones fashioned his country's naval war strategy. He strengthened the impact of the country's weak coastal defense gunboats by concentrating them at the most important ports and regions, including New York, New Orleans, the Delaware and Chesapeake Bays, and the coast of Georgia. He favored single warship cruises of *guerre de course*—raids on commercial shipping—and wrote to his captains saying that his intention was "to dispatch all our public ships, now in port, as soon as possible, in such positions as may be best adapted to destroy the commerce of the enemy." He felt sloops were the best type of ship for this activity and pushed for their construction. The Secretary wanted to avoid combat between the small number of US war vessels and the superior British fleet. He also put together a sound program to build up American naval power on the Great Lakes. During his tenure as navy administrator, Jones presided over a proposed expansion of the US Navy, as per Congressional legislation passed early in 1813, which envisioned adding six 74-gun capital ships, six 44-gun frigates, and six armed sloops to the fleet. It was an impressive target.

✦ ✦ ✦

"I would give all our prizes," wrote the commander of HMS *Shannon* to his wife on September 14, 1812, "for an American frigate." For months, Captain Philip Vere Broke and his ship—the 38-gun *Shannon*—had "sauntered about off Boston," blockading that port,

British Captain Philip Broke leads the boarding party that captures the Chesapeake.

and as his letter stressed, he was eager for a fight. On May 3, 1813, the USS *President*, accompanied by USS *Congress*, broke out of Boston harbor, even though that port had been under the watchful eye of a powerful British blockading force including *Shannon*. The escape of the two American vessels left one US frigate still in the harbor—the 36-gun USS *Chesapeake* under Captain James Lawrence. It was the *Chesapeake* that Broke was eager to fight.

In order to lure the American ship out of Boston, Broke wrote Lawrence a crafty and insulting letter challenging him to come out and engage in single combat with *Shannon*. As further inducement, Broke sent away all friendly ships in the area to assure his opponent it would be a one-on-one fight. Lawrence never received the challenge but, on his own volition, left Boston on June 1 and headed straight for *Shannon* seeking battle. As *Chesapeake*

Captain James Lawrence, commander of the Chesapeake.

approached at 5:00pm, Broke told his crew, "Don't try to dismast her [*Chesapeake*]. Fire into her quarters. Kill the men and the ship is yours." *Chesapeake* had the weather gauge and soon came up to her opponent, but instead of maneuvering to rake her stern, the Yankee came abreast of *Shannon*. At almost 6:00pm, the two vessels commenced trading heavy broadsides as *Chesapeake* inched parallel to her opponent. Soon both ships were damaged and Lawrence was wounded. His ship's headsail sheets were blown away, causing her to lift up into the wind, out of control, presenting her stern to the enemy and making it impossible for her to train more than a few cannon on her foe.

When *Chesapeake's* quarter galley collapsed on Shannon's bow, Broke ordered a 50-man boarding party to follow him on to the stricken American ship. The Yankee crew was also assembling a boarding party but the British captain moved quicker, and in minutes cleared *Chesapeake's* entire main deck. In the brutal hand-to-hand struggle, Broke was twice badly wounded by pistol ball and cutlass stroke, but was saved from fatal injury by the silk top hat he habitually wore. Before the boarding, Lawrence was mortally wounded, and before he was taken below decks he called to one of his officers, "Tell the men to fire faster. Don't give up the ship." But exhortations were no match against the British assault, and 15 minutes after the battle commenced, *Chesapeake* surrendered. On June 6, she and the *Shannon* entered Halifax. The myth of American frigate invincibility had been dispelled by superior British gunnery. The bloody affair between *Chesapeake* and *Shannon* cost the Americans 47 killed, and 98 wounded, and the British 33 killed and 50 wounded.

✦ ✦ ✦

The last six months of 1813 presented few bright spots for the US Navy. Captures were few and even getting out of port was difficult for American ships. After John Rodgers slipped out of Boston harbor on the *President*, he sailed for the West Indies, the Azores and Norway. He returned to Newport, Rhode Island that September after taking 13 prizes, including a small warship. *Congress* separated from *President* after leaving Boston. Her eight-month cruise bagged only four British ships. Stephen Decatur, leaving New York harbor in late May with *United States, Macedonian* and *Hornet,* was forced to run for New London, Connecticut, in the face of superior numbers of British vessels, and was promptly blockaded there. *Constitution* was trapped in Boston, *Constellation* at Norfolk, Virginia, and *Adams* in Chesapeake Bay.

Echoes of the glory days of 1812 returned with news of the exploits of the 14-gun USS *Enterprise*, whose commander, Lieutenant William Ward Burrows II, sailing from Portsmouth, New Hampshire, had orders "to proceed to sea on a cruise along the coast [of Maine]" to protect the coastal trade being "interrupted by small cruisers of the enemy." On September 5, Burrows sighted the British 14-gun brig HMS *Boxer*, under Commander Samuel Blyth. Both ships were evenly matched. After a few hours of maneuvering out of cannon range, Burrows made straight for *Boxer* "with intention to bring her to close action." Both vessels held their fire until they were running alongside one another at ten yards distance. The first exchange of cannon killed Blyth and mortally wounded Burrows. After a

Death of Captain Lawrence on board the Chesapeake, *his last instructions being: "Tell the men to fire faster. Don't give up the ship."*

15-minute duel, *Boxer's* rigging and topmast were gone, there was three feet of water in her hold, and she had ceased firing. The British vessel surrendered and was towed to Portland. The fight had cost the Americans three killed and 14 wounded, while *Boxer* lost four dead and 18 injured.

Another American warship making a name for herself during a year of disappointment for the United States Navy was USS *Argus*, a 16-gun brig under Lieutenant Henry Allen. Leaving New York in June, Allen embarked on a commerce-destroying mission around the British Isles. In those waters, he captured 21 enemy craft, which he then burned. In response to the American's amazing success, the Admiralty sent HMS *Pelican* after her, under Commander John F. Maples. On August 15 they met off the Irish Coast, and although the opponents were closely matched, *Argus* was pummeled into surrendering after a brutal 45-minute close-action contest that might have gone either way. *Argus* lost six killed and 18 wounded, including the fatally wounded Allen, *Pelican* two dead, five wounded.

A third Yankee warship did considerable mischief during the last part of 1813. Captain David Porter, Jr. and his 32-gun frigate USS *Essex* had been on the prowl since it left the Delaware Capes in October 1812. Its mission was to engage in commerce raiding in the South Atlantic. Failing to rendezvous with William Bainbridge off the east coast of the United States, and then Brazil, Porter went off on his own, rounding Cape Horn and reaching Chile in March. He then set himself the mission of attacking the British Pacific whaling fleet, as well as English privateers stalking the US whaling flotilla.

Between April and October 1813, Porter took 12 enemy whalers and disrupted

British whaling operations in the Galapagos Islands. After travelling to the Marquesas Islands, Porter arrived at Valparaiso, Chile, in February 1813. On March 28, after being cornered in the anchorage by two British warships for six weeks—the 36-gun *Phoebe* and 28-gun *Cherub*—Porter attempted to slip away, but lost his main topmast in a heavy squall. He was forced to enter a small bay outside Valparaiso where he was fired on by his opponent's longer-ranged guns. After enduring two and a half hours of punishing bombardment, the *Essex* surrendered, having lost 58 killed and 65 wounded. The British lost five killed and ten wounded.

✦   ✦   ✦

The year 1814 saw a continuance of the war at sea. Evading the British outside Boston harbor, John Steward sailed USS *Constitution* to Guyana in January. For the next two months, he took only two merchantmen and an armed schooner. On one occasion, he attempted to overtake an enemy frigate, on another he escaped from two such vessels. In early April, he returned to Boston.

In late April, the first American sloop-of-war, the 22-gun USS *Frolic* set off for Cuba but was run down and captured. The sloop USS *Peacock* was much luckier, leaving New York to cruise to the Caribbean, where it captured 14 freighters. She also captured HMS *Epervier*, an 18-gun British brig, after a 45-minute duel, before returning to New York in

US officers on board the Chesapeake *surrender their swords to Captain Broke.*

October. USS *Wasp*, a 22-gunner under Johnston Blakely, set sail from Portsmouth in May. During her cruise, which took her to the English Channel and South America, she took 13 merchant vessels and defeated two British brigs—the *Reindeer* and *Avon*—before disappearing, mostly likely falling victim to a hurricane.

During 1815, naval activity on the high seas continued, even though the final peace treaty between the United States and Great Britain was taking shape. On January 14, 1815, Decatur tried to leave New York harbor when his ship, USS *President*, ran aground, causing considerable damage and retarding her sailing ability. Next day, *President* was overtaken by three enemy ships, one of which, the 50-gun HMS *Endymion*, engaged her. *President's* heavy broadsides soon reduced the British vessel to a wreck. However, other enemy frigates came on the scene, and after belching their devastating iron broadsides into the struggling *President*, Decatur was forced to strike his colors.

Captain Charles Stewart, on the USS *Constitution* at this time, was out at sea, having departed Boston in mid-December 1814. By February 14, she was off the Spanish coast where she fought and captured two British warships—the 30-gun frigate *Cyane* and 18-gun sloop *Levant*—in the same battle. The last confrontation at sea occurred between the 18-gun USS *Hornet* and 18-gun HMS *Penguin* on March 23 in the South Atlantic. Within 25 minutes, the well-aimed fire of the American crippled her adversary.

Bitter battle between the two frigates USS Chesapeake *and HMS* Shannon *outside of Boston on June 1, 1813.*

British naval gunner c1813. Painting by Bryan Fosten.

✦ ✦ ✦

As Secretary of the Navy, Jones wanted American privateers, in the form of ships, brigs, schooners, sloops and smaller craft, to harry the British commerce fleet. The result was the American capture of almost 1,400 vessels during the war. In contrast, warships of the US Navy took only 254 commercial and military craft during the conflict. With opportunities for legitimate shipping almost gone due to the British blockade, and the presence of British warships at sea, the American merchant marine turned to privateering with gusto. They often travelled in packs. Unlike the boxy bulk carriers of the European merchant marine, sharp-lined American brigs and schooners of less than 300 tons made good improvised privateers. Many of these privateers were large ships mounting 20 to 30 cannon. The seas around the British Isles proved to be some of the most lucrative hunting grounds for these American raiders.

Contrary to popular opinion, the successful privateer was in the minority. Of the 525 licensed privateers, only 207 ever took a prize. The most successful was the *America*, out of Salem, Massachusetts, which captured 41 enemy ships. Most holders of "letters of marque and reprisal" were traders whose main profit came from cargoes that successfully ran through the blockade, the letter of marque merely giving them the right to seize an enemy merchant vessel should the opportunity arise. It was a risky enterprise, as 148 American holders of letters of marque were captured, as well as two thirds of all their prize crews.

Overall, the effect of American privateers on British commercial trade was only moderate, with the number of British ships and tonnage actually rising during the war. In 1812, the British merchant marine had 20,637 ships, representing 2,263,000 tons of shipping. By 1815, the number of vessels had increased to 21,869, with total tonnage rising to 2,478,000. British imports and exports also grew from $60,000,000 and $48,000,000 in 1812, to $90,000,000 and $59,000,000, respectively, by 1815. America's *guerre de course* did, however, influence the final peace treaty. It softened Britain's terms for peace in light of the potential harm America could do in the future to her commercial sea trade in the form of lost profits, increased taxes and high shipping insurance rates.

On the other side of the balance sheet, by mid-1813, all along the American East Coast, foreign trade was sharply reduced and customs revenues dried up. "Commerce is becoming very slack," reported John Hollins of Baltimore on April 8, "no arrivals from abroad, & nothing going to sea but sharp [fast] vessels." It was not just the foreign carrying trade that was affected, but coastal commerce between the states as well. The British blockade—the "Wooden Walls" placed off the US shore by the Royal Navy—was tightening its grip.

First instituted after war was declared, the British blockade of the US coastline was the classic strategy of the dominant sea power designed to prevent enemy warships and commerce raiders from going to sea and returning to port, and the wider economic blockade aimed at suppressing all trade. Plagued from start to finish by lack of resources to make it 100 percent effective, the blockade still had a great deal of success. Regardless of Admiral Warren's inadequate force, the blockade managed in 1812 to capture 240 American ships trying to slip out to sea, the vast majority of which were merchantmen engaged in normal commerce. In 1813, the blockade became more potent; squadron-size forces combining a 74-gun man-of-war with a frigate or more were off every major American harbor to keep the dreaded US Navy's frigates in port, or vulnerable to defeat in battle if they dared emerge from harbor. Small shallow draft vessels were also present to chase coasters and privateers, as well as American gunboats. The latter routinely attacked conventional Royal Navy ships operating in the restricted waters of bays and estuaries where they could not easily maneuver.

But mixed objectives by the Admiralty hindered the blockade's results. The focus on destroying American naval forces through the diversion of fleet resources to Chesapeake and Delaware Bays under Admiral George Cockburn, and the huge number of ships used in the effort to trap enemy warships in port, such as Decatur's squadron at New York, or the *Chesapeake* in Boston, left holes in the blockade that, militarily, more than offset the victories gained over American warships either defeated in combat or locked up in port.

During the opening months of 1814, the blockade seemed almost nonexistent since Warren had to leave much of the coast unguarded due to the Chesapeake Campaign, and continued chronic lack of ships. However, enough blockaders remained, allowing commercial interdiction that proved a great success. Unarmed merchants no longer ran the blockade, coastal trade had almost entirely ceased, and neutrals no longer legally entered American ports.

Spring saw an increase to 85 British warships available for duty in American waters as a result of the abdication of Napoleon in April. The new head of the North American Station, Vice Admiral Sir Alexander Cochrane, brought increased vigor, and more men and ships, to the blockade effort. Yet the flow of enemy warships and privateers continued from the southern ports, since the admiral concentrated his resources from the Chesapeake Bay northward to the previously unblockaded New England coast. The southern coast did not receive British attention until August 1814, when several squadrons were sent down there. By the end of 1814 there were 120 Royal Navy ships, including those at Jamaica, manning the blockade. In January 1815, the Royal Navy got serious when it seized Cumberland and St. Simons Islands and created a base for disrupting coastal trade traffic.

Although extremely costly to American trade during the last two war years, the British blockade, declared in four separate stages, remained less than fully efficient during the war due to the lack of adequate numbers of men and ships, divergent British objectives, the hazards of the sea, British commitments worldwide, and the aggressive American response to it in the form of privateers. However, with conflict in Europe finally ending in mid-1815, Great Britain prepared to devote massive naval assets to the American War, which would have included enough ships and manpower to completely strangle US ocean and coastal commerce if it had the chance to be applied.

✦ ✦ ✦

The notice in Baltimore's *Weekly Register* in late 1813 was quite explicit in its offer of a $1,000 reward for the head of a "notorious incendiary and infamous scoundrel, and violator of all laws, human divine, the British admiral COCKBURN—or, *five hundred* dollars for each ear, on delivery." The bounty was placed in retaliation for the raids through spring and summer that year conducted by the British under Cockburn, by that time the most hated man in America, charged with every perceived atrocity committed on the East Coast.

George Cockburn, born April 22, 1772, made Lieutenant in the Royal Navy at age 21, thereafter commanding a sloop-of-war, then frigates in the Mediterranean and West Indies. In 1812 he was named Vice Admiral and assigned to be second-in-command to Admiral Warren with the North American Station. Upon arrival in the American theater, he was ordered by Warren to conduct combined operations—a natural adjunct to the British blockade—in the Chesapeake Bay region, designed to destroy enemy supplies and privateer

*Sir George Cockburn, the British naval commander who conducted a series of destructive
raids along the East Coast of America.*

nests, as well as bringing political pressure to bear on the US government by attacking an area which was very pro-war but might change its tune if hit hard by the conflict.

This siege of the American coast was possible due to the neglect that the Jefferson and Madison administrations had given to coastal and harbor defense, which was for the most part left to ineffectual gunboats, and the difficulties of navigation that was hoped would keep enemy vessels out. On land, the situation was no better, there being few regular infantry, and fewer artillery units on hand to defend coastal towns. Untrained local militiamen were ultimately depended upon, but most of the time they fled in the face of even minor British incursions.

Supported by conventional warships and smaller vessels able to penetrate the inland waterways, plus 380 sailors and Royal Marines, Cockburn conducted a campaign of burning and looting communities of anything that might aid the American cause. Frenchtown, Maryland, on the Elk River was plundered on April 29; then Havre-de-Grace, Maryland, at the entrance of the Susquehanna River was burned, even though it had no strategic importance. The towns of Georgetown and Fredericktown were torched next on May 6, after a half hour skirmish between 80 militia and British Marines involving Congreve rockets fired into the village. While these exploits cost the defenders hundreds of thousands of dollars in lost property, the British suffered only a handful of wounded for their efforts.

Moving to Virginia, Cockburn attacked Carney Island, near Norfolk, on June 22 by amphibious assault with 1,300 marines and sailors. The attack was repulsed by American naval and military forces, with a loss to the British of 177 killed, wounded and missing. The British were more successful in taking Hampton, Virginia, on June 25, but the resultant assaults, murder and looting of American civilians created an outrage in both the US and Britain.

Intending to keep a strong permanent presence in the Chesapeake Bay region, in early August, Kent Island, Maryland, was occupied by the British and used as a staging area for attacks on Annapolis, Baltimore, Washington, DC and the eastern shore of Maryland. The punitive raids spread panic and fury throughout the area, and would continue in 1814, but no matter how destructive their results they ultimately proved a strategic distraction and a diversion of limited British resources needed to complete their military and economic blockade.

When it could not make America sue for peace in 1813, the British lost faith in the combination of blockade and pinprick inland raids to get its enemy to end the conflict. The British government then, with the prospect of massive reinforcements of troops from Europe due to the fall of Napoleon, changed strategic course and determined to go on the offensive. With its newfound military strength, it would launch concerted drives on the American national capital and Baltimore from the Chesapeake area, and advance into New York State from Canada. This new strategy, it was assumed, would either win the war outright, or at the very least gain Britain favorable terms when peace was finally arranged.

A soldier's wife at Fort Niagara. Courtesy of the Library of Congress

CHAPTER EIGHT

The Niagara Front Ablaze

—◦◦◦—

ACCORDING TO *NILES' WEEKLY REGISTER*, "GEN WILKINSON SEEMS TO HAVE exposed his life with great prodigality," during the fight at Lacolle Mills in March1814. That claim was an exaggeration, but what was not was the pitiful performance of the latest American advance into Canada.

In late January 1814, James Wilkinson was ordered by the US Secretary of War, John Armstrong, to remove his diseased and frostbitten army from their encampment at French Mills to Plattsburg, New York. A month later, the Major-General made his last military effort by attacking an isolated enemy position five miles beyond the Canadian border at a road crossing over the Lacolle River. The object of the attack was a large stone mill garrisoned by 180 British regulars, militia, and marines serving as an outpost on the direct route from Lake Champlain to Montreal. Against this vulnerable target, Wilkinson sent 4,000 men and 11 artillery pieces. On March 30, after over two hours shooting up the place—without making any impression on the defenses and losing 254 casualties to the British 61—the Americans trudged back through the snow to Plattsburg. On April 11, his military reputation ruined by the fiasco at Lacolle, Wilkinson was relieved of his military responsibilities. It was the start of a long overdue reorganization of the American army high command.

In what was Armstrong's most valuable service during the war, the Secretary appointed three new Major-Generals, all excellent choices. The first, George Izard, raised in South Carolina, entered the United States Army in 1794 as a Lieutenant of engineers. He was the only American general in the War of 1812 who had a formal military education, having enrolled in the French Ecole du Genie in 1795. A Captain eight years later, he left the service as the US Army shrunk under President Jefferson. In 1812, he rejoined the army as a Colonel, and made Brigadier-General in 1813. He performed well during Hampton's advance to Montreal in late 1813, and in January next year was promoted to Major-General, becoming at the age of 38 the most senior US army commander along the Canadian frontier.

Jacob Jennings Brown was the second Major-General named. Although having no military training before the war, he was a man of action and had shown a combativeness that was both effective and inspiring. Made Brigadier in 1813, he distinguished himself in Wilkinson's Montreal Campaign.

Andrew Jackson, a transplanted South Carolinian to Tennessee, born March 15, 1767, was the third appointee. He had fought as a boy during the American Revolutionary War, and prior to the War of 1812 was a lawyer, United States Congressman and US Sen-

Major-General Andrew Jackson— future President of the United States— first distinguished himself fighting Creek Indians during the War of 1812. Portrait by Thomas Sully.

ator, a state Supreme Court justice, and militia Major-General. During the summer of 1813, he cobbled together a militia force and conducted successful campaigns against the Creek Indians for which he was made a Brigadier-General in the US Army in 1814. On May 1, he was named Major-General in the Regular Army as a replacement for William H. Harrison, who had resigned from that service due to simmering differences with the Secretary of War.

In addition to the new Major-Generals, Armstrong appointed seven additional Brigadier- Generals during 1814: Alexander Macomb, Thomas Adams Smith, Daniel Bissell, Edmund Pendleton Gaines, Winfield Scott, Eleazar Wheelock Ripley, and Thomas Parker. The first six had distinguished themselves during the early stages of the war. Parker served as a staff officer during the conflict.

Prior to the command shake-up in the American Army initiated by Armstrong, Sir George Prevost made changes in the British military leadership responsible for the defense of Canada. In December 1813, Gordon Drummond was made civil and military administrator of Upper Canada, while Generals de Rottenburg, Vincent and Proctor were assigned to command troops in Upper Canada, Kingston, and York, respectively, and Sheaffe returned to England.

Lieutenant-General Drummond was born in Quebec on September 27, 1772. Joining the British Army in 1789, he attained his lieutenant-general's rank in 1811. His combat experience included action in Egypt, Holland and the West Indies. A dynamic leader, persistence, aggressiveness and determination were all hallmarks of his soldierly qualities. Seconding Drummond was Phineas Riall, an officer in the British Army since 1794. Made a Major-General in 1812, he was posted to Canada as military governor of the Montreal District. A 38-year-old Irishman, his previous combat experience was limited to campaigning in the West Indies. Brave, and bold, bordering on rash, in December1813 he conducted punitive raids on the American side of the Niagara River, defeating large contingents of opposing militia, and burning Buffalo and Black Rock, New York in retaliation for Yankee depredations on Canadian soil. When Drummond assumed control of Upper Canada, Riall was put in charge of the Niagara frontier.

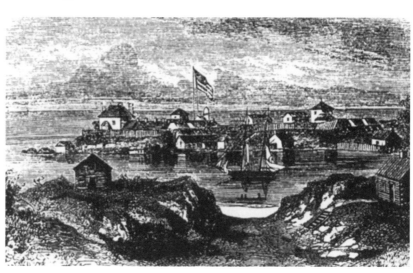

Fort Niagara on Lake Ontario, as viewed from Fort George. A strategically important target for the Americans.

As in the previous year, Armstrong made the centerpiece of campaigning in 1814 in the East the capture of Kingston—the key to British naval control of Lake Ontario, as well as the chokepoint for men and material moving from Lower to Upper Canada. Toward that end, he issued two orders to Jacob Brown, who had been placed in charge of the Niagara Front. The first, concocted as a ruse to mislead the British, directed Brown to recover Fort Niagara and Fort George; the second, and the one Armstrong really wanted Brown to execute, ordered the capture of Kingston. Unintended, Brown fell for Armstrong's ruse, thinking he really had been ordered to take the forts. When it was pointed out to him by

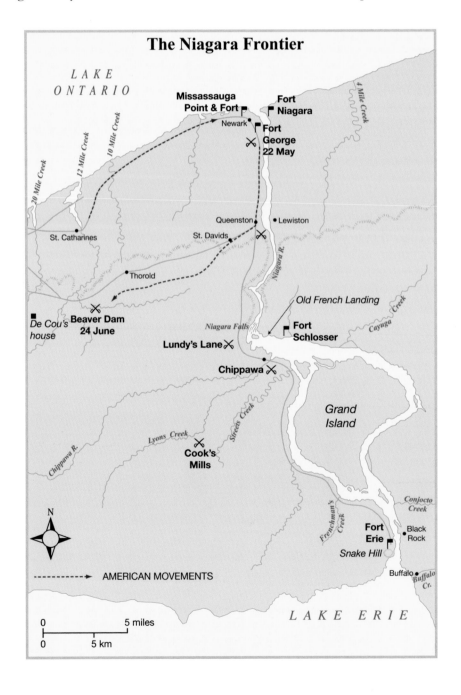

one of his subordinates what Armstrong really wanted him to do, Brown requested assistance from Commodore Chauncey for an army and navy descent on that town. However, the latter refused, claiming, mistakenly, that his squadron was inferior to Yeo's, thus making it impossible, in the Commodore's view, for the American flotilla to leave Sackets Harbor.

Chauncey's attitude was an example of the failure of US military leaders to integrate land and water forces in a combined enterprise designed to achieve a decisive goal. The near loss of his base at Sackets Harbor in 1813 resulted in the naval commander's focus being first to safeguard his operational base, second to defeat his opponent in a waterborne engagement, thus relegating cooperation with the army in seizing Kingston, or cutting the St. Lawrence River supply line, to last place in his strategic calculations. What Chauncey settled for was a naval arms race that suited his opponent, since avoidance of battle gave the strategic victory to the British on Lake Ontario. Further, Chauncey was reluctant to escort supply and troop transport craft with war vessels. This would reduce the number of ships available for fleet actions, which he insisted he wanted but in fact avoided. Neither did Chauncey want to stray far from his base since this could invite enemy attacks.

As the naval arms race on Lake Ontario accelerated in 1814, it took on a life of its own. In April, the 62-gun frigate USS *Superior* was completed, giving the US a rough parity with the British, who had that month launched two new frigates of their own. The 42-gun USS *Mohawk* was launched in June, giving Chauncey the edge over his rival until HMS *St. Lawrence*—a 102-gun ship-of-the-line—was put in the water in September. But the increased tonnage and number of cannon on the ships never brought about the decisive battle that Chauncey claimed he desired, and Yeo refused to engage in. Its most important impact was to preclude American land and water cooperation, immeasurably aiding the British in their defense of Canada.

✦　✦　✦

"If you left the [Sackets] Harbor with a competent force for its defense," wrote John Armstrong to General Jacob Brown on March 20, 1814, "go on and prosper. Good consequences are sometimes the result of mistakes." Thus the Secretary of War, realizing his ploy to outwit the British had instead confused his own subordinate, left the choice of the objective for the 1814 campaign in the east in Brown's hands. As a result, Brown started to prepare a plan that entailed the US Lake Erie squadron moving his force to the south shore of the Niagara Peninsula. From there he would go north across Grand River, take Burlington Heights, and then clear the rest of the peninsula by capturing Forts Erie, George and Niagara. Complicating the plan was the Madison administration's insistence on retaking Mackinac Island, thus depriving Brown of 1,000 men, and support from the Lake Erie squadron to transport his troops and supplies.

While Brown spent time at Sackets Harbor strengthening its defenses, American troops on the Niagara frontier, under his principal subordinate, Winfield Scott, underwent extensive training near Buffalo, New York. Captain Rufus McIntire, 3rd US Artillery Regiment, who had served under Scott during the Chrysler's Farm campaign, felt confident in

Scott's ability as a trainer and combat leader and wrote, "If it be possible to meet the enemy I know Scott will manage to meet him if he can do it on anything like equal ground." Drill, discipline and motivation were the essence of Scott's training regime, and that focus would make his regulars equal to their British counterpart.

In early May, Armstrong gave his approval to the latter's proposed offensive, but on June 9 he ordered the scheme suspended until Chauncey gained command of Lake Ontario. In the meantime, Armstrong suggested to Brown that he use his force to clear the Niagara River all the way to Fort George. Thinking along these same lines, Brown wrote to Gaines of his predicament, acknowledging, "I do not know that I am to be supported by the Fleet of either Lake but I intend to enter the Enemy's Country about the first of July." Brown and Armstrong knew that without Chauncey's help, an American advance beyond Burlington Heights was unlikely. As it was, the Yankee Commodore chose to stick close to his base at Sackets Harbor and gave no aid to the army in the forthcoming campaign. Consequently, the General decided to cross the Niagara directly in the face of the enemy in a replay of Smyth's attack in 1812. His force, designated the Left Division, consisted of 5,358 regulars and about 600 Native American allies. An additional 1,500 soldiers under Gaines garrisoned Sackets Harbor.

"The views of His Majesty's Government respecting the mode of conducting the War with America," wrote Sir George Prevost early in 1814, "do not justify my exposing too much on one stake." However, he always left open the door for what he called "daring enterprises with disproportionate means" that even if unsuccessful would not endanger Lower Canada. While the Americans struggled to formulate a coherent campaign plan for 1814, the British, adhering to Prevost's defensive philosophy, watched and waited.

Prevost's passive strategy was not an easy one for Gordon Drummond to accept, while he formulated a defensive plan to thwart the coming American operation. It consisted of spreading his forces thin along the Niagara River with small troop concentrations at Forts Niagara, George and Erie, and Burlington Heights. Although courting defeat in detail if the enemy struck swiftly and in force, it would give the British time to react to their opponent's moves, as well as allowing them to slow done the Americans at key points. Drummond took the risk based on his belief that his opponent was going to focus on the recapture of Fort Niagara, and his contempt for American martial abilities based on their past performance in the east.

To implement his program, in March Drummond ordered Riall to use his 2,700 men on the Niagara Peninsula to maintain a thin screen of forces along the 30-mile-long Niagara River, while concentrating his main strength at Forts Niagara and George. He directed his subordinate to place defense forces on the Chippawa River, the largest water course on the peninsula, and Fort Erie to create a defensive shield, but one from which Riall could make "a rapid movement from Chippawa to support the Detachments on the Right [west and south], and to oppose any descent made from above [south of] Chippawa [River]." In other words, if opportunity arose, Riall was encouraged to seize the initiative by attacking the enemy. While Riall headed the Right Division, Drummond led the Left

Port of Buffalo on Lake Erie. American troops on the Niagara frontier underwent extensive training near here.

Division of four regular regiments that defended Kingston and eastward to the border with Lower Canada.

Around 2:00am on Sunday, July 3, General Brown launched his invasion of the Niagara Peninsula. His 1st Brigade under Winfield Scott, with part of Ripley's 2nd Brigade, landed on the Canadian shore above Fort Erie, while the rest of the 2nd Brigade hit the beach below the fort. Brown's intention was to encircle the enemy position and then pound it into submission with his artillery. As the American small boats neared shore, they were fired upon by a British picket from the 100th Foot Regiment. The fire was both accurate and "galling." To inspire his men, Scott jumped into the water to lead them ashore but almost drowned in the surf.

Except for Scott's mishap, the landing of the 1st and part of the 2nd Brigades went well, and when Brown crossed over at dawn those units were preparing to move against the fort. The landing below the post, however, was delayed by a lack of boats and fog, and not completed until 6:00am. Brown ordered Major Thomas Jesup's 25th US Infantry Regiment to close on the fort and prevent the garrison from escaping. As Jesup's men approached it, they were hit by artillery fire, which wounded four of their number. As one member of the unit recalled, they expected that the regiment would have to "carry it [the fort] by storm as it was supposed to be well manned and fortified." But early that afternoon, as American 18-pounders were being wheeled into position before the post, its commander, Major Thomas Buck, surrendered the garrison's 137 men and three guns.

By 8:00am, Riall, at Fort George, got word of the American crossing. He ordered five companies of the 1st Foot Regiment, a squadron of the 19th Light Dragoons, and Captain James Mackonochie's eight-gun battery to follow him to Chippawa. The 2nd Lincoln Militia Regiment and the 300 Grand River Indian allies, under their leader, John Norton, were also told to move there. Riall's third regular unit, the 8th Foot Regiment, on its way from York, was directed to hurry its march to Chippawa. Meanwhile, word of the American incursion was sent to Lieutenant Colonel Thomas Pearson in charge of the Chippawa position, as well as commander of Riall's British light troops and Indians.

The British base at Chippawa was a strong one. The Chippawa River, which split the village in two, was a "dull muddy river running through flat, swampy country" 250-feet wide, spanned by a narrow wooden bridge running into the Niagara River. The bridge was shielded on the north bank by a line of entrenchments and a redoubt, making a frontal attack on it problematical. The position could not be outflanked to the east due to the Niagara River, and was difficult to turn from the west over the marshy and obstructed terrain in that direction.

Not knowing that Fort Erie had surrendered, Riall wished to attack the Americans while they were besieging the fort, but elected to wait until his 8th Foot was up. On July 4, Brown ordered Scott to march north from Fort Erie with his brigade, some artillery, and Captain Samuel Harris' squadron of the 2nd Light Dragoons to the Chippawa River. Brown followed Scott with the rest of the Left Division that afternoon.

Four miles from Fort Erie, at Frenchman's Creek, Scott ran into Pearson's composite battalion of regular light troops, dragoons and two artillery pieces. As Scott prepared to force a crossing, the British pulled out after discharging a few musket and artillery rounds at the invaders. For the next 14 hot, dusty miles, creek after creek, Pearson delayed the bluecoat advance until they came up to Street's Creek, the last stream before the Chippawa. Hoping to capture the British guns, a company from the 9th US Infantry Regiment crossed the stream to the west and prepared to take the enemy pieces, but they were charged by the British dragoons. Seeing the danger, the infantry ran for the shelter of a nearby farmhouse and were able to beat off the mounted attack. Later in the day, Pearson, now joined by Norton's Indians, crossed to the north bank of the Chippawa River. At dusk, after approaching Chippawa, and realizing he could not take the bridge, Scott went into camp south of Street's Creek. At midnight, Brown, Ripley's brigade, and the division's artillery and trains joined Scott after a 15-mile rain-soaked march.

The contest next day would be fought on flat ground called the "plain," a convex arc two miles long between the Chippawa River and Street's Creek. The terrain closest to the Niagara was meadowland covered in waist-high grass partitioned by fences. Three-quarters of a mile from the Niagara lay a dense, cluttered forest. Projecting from the wood, a tongue of timber 400 yards long, stretching to within a quarter of a mile west of the Niagara, formed a natural defile in the middle of this normally open area. During most of the morning of July 5, British snipers harassed the Americans near their camp from the woodland, and according to Captain Benjamin Ropes, 21st US Infantry Regiment, who was posted on guard in the area, "we had considerable Skirmishing [in] the forenoon."

American gray-clad troops advance at the battle of Chippawa on July 5, 1814. At first, the British thought they were militia who would be easily routed, only realising their mistake too late. Painting by H. Charles McBarron.

Reports from his militia and Indians engaged with the American sentries convinced Riall that he was facing only 2,000 Americans and that the remainder of Brown's army was besieging Fort Erie. That assumption, as well as the arrival of his entire command, about 1,400 regulars, 200 militia, 300 Indians, and his artillery at Chippawa, determined him to attack.

With the strip of woodland blocking his view of British preparations at Chippawa, Brown had no idea of an impending enemy assault. He therefore rode south to bring up New York Militia Brigadier-General Peter Buell Porter's 1,000-man mixed Pennsylvania militia and the Seneca Indian 3rd Brigade, which had crossed the Niagara the night before and was marching to the American bivouac below Street's Creek.

Porter, 41-years-old, was an attorney and War Hawk in the US House of Representatives from 1809 to 1813. A Brigadier-General in the New York militia, early in the war he was critical of the senior officers of the US Army. Untrained in military matters prior to the conflict, he became a brave and competent practitioner of that art during the Niagara Campaign of 1814.

On orders, at 3:00pm, Porter gathered 500 of his militia and 56 regulars, as he wrote later, to "drive off the hostile Indians who had been firing at our pickets" from the wood surrounding the American camp. Forming a skirmish line three quarters of a mile long, preceded by Indian scouts, Porter's men entered the woods just south of the American encampment. Immediately, the opposing Indian auxiliaries made contact and fierce combat between them commenced, with the British-allied Natives being pushed back. Suddenly Porter's Indians came rushing toward the rear after they had come up against a solid line of Redcoats. They had blundered into Riall's attack.

At 3:00pm, Riall had ordered his men to the south bank of the Chippawa, his main force remaining in column while Pearson's light troops—2nd Lincoln Militia and 200 of Norton's Indians—anchored his right. The clash with Porter's command in the woods soon followed. A series of American musket volleys decimated the Canadian militia and Grand River Indians, but the disciplined fire of Pearson's regular light companies drove the Americans through the woods back to their camp.

Earlier, Riall's main force had marched down the road adjacent to the Niagara River and deployed on the northern edge of the plain: the 100th Foot on the left, then the 1st Foot, with the 8th behind the 1st, the 19th Light Dragoons on the road to the rear of the 100th, with artillery detachments on each wing. Riall was confident of the battle's outcome, supposedly saying that his opponents were "a set of cowardly untrained men who will not stand the bayonet."

Detecting this enemy move, Brown who was in the plain, ordered up Scott's 1,300 men, uniformed in gray, not the standard blue US Army uniform, to meet the enemy coming down the river highway. As Scott's troops crossed Street's Creek, they came under British artillery fire but managed to form a battle line—from right to left, Captain Nathan Towson's three 12-pounders on the river road, then the combined 9th/22 US Infantry, Ropes' company of the 21st Infantry, and finally the 11th US Infantry Regiment. Viewing this well executed maneuver under fire, Riall realized he was not facing gray-clad militia and exclaimed, "Damn, these are regulars." Private George Ferguson of the 100th, also saw the American line forming flawlessly and decided that the Americans facing them were "unquestionably well disciplined troops." A short artillery duel then ensued, until Riall ordered an attack on the American line.

At 4:30pm, the British 1st and 100th went straight at the enemy, while the 8th was moving up some distance behind and to their right while keeping an eye on the US 25th Regiment moving to the British right. The British movement masked their supporting artillery and relieved the waiting Americans of the punishing fire it had been delivering. As the three battalions moved forward, a growing gap developed between the 1st, 100th and the 8th Foot. Scott saw this and ordered the US 11th Infantry on his left to throw forward its left flank companies to fire on the exposed British right. This caused severe losses to the British. When these two battalions came within 100 yards of the American line, Scott ordered the Americans to commence firing. The Redcoats halted under the withering enemy musket and artillery fire, and began exchanging musket volleys with their opponents.

It was 4:00pm when Brown ordered the 2nd Brigade's 21st Infantry to move from camp, enter the woods and strike the British right. Unfortunately, the regiment never got into the fight due to the difficulties crossing Street's Creek and moving through the woods. Meanwhile, the 25th US moved to its left and engaged the British light troops who were harassing the American left flank from the edge of the woods. According to Captain George Howard, the 25th came "within grinning distance," when its Colonel ordered, "Halt, ready, fire three rounds and charge." The enemy fled, with the Americans following until they gained the right flank of the 8th Foot, which was preparing to face the onrushing 25th. Its independent brawl with the US 25th prevented it from aiding the 1st and 100th Foot in their fight with Scott's main line.

As the two Redcoat battalions and the Americans blazed away at each other, the British battalion leaders, Lieutenant-Colonels George Hay and John Gordon, of the 100th and 1st Foot, respectively, attempted without success to get their men to charge their opponents. Hay later wrote, "Despite my best efforts I could not get them to advance." Both battalion leaders were soon felled by enemy bullets. Meanwhile, additional American artillery came into play as newly arrived guns were inserted between the 11th and 9/22 Regiments. With losses mounting, his men barely holding their positions, and no possibility of a decisive bayonet charge by them to clear the enemy from the field, Riall ordered a retreat. The 1st and 100th Foot retraced their path northward, then formed into column on the river road—covered by the 8th Foot and the 19th Light Dragoons—and proceeded to cross to the north bank of the Chippawa. Norton's Indians in the woods followed suit.

Scott and Porter followed the British to the south bank of the Chippawa. It was 6:30pm when Brown deemed the hour too late to attempt to storm the British position across the river. "Cousin Jonathan" had defeated "John Bull" after a bloody three and a half hour struggle. The cost paid was 58 dead, 241 wounded, and 19 missing, including Indians, on the American side; 148 killed, 321 wounded, and 46 missing for the British. The Americans estimated British Native losses at 87.

✦ ✦ ✦

On July 8, Riall decamped from Chippawa after Brown gained a position to flank him from the west. On July 23, the British moved to Twenty Mile Creek after leaving strong garrisons in Forts George and Niagara, while the Americans, unable to reduce either place due to the absence of a siege train, which Chauncey's fleet would not transport to the peninsula,

SOLDIERS on a march to BUFFALO.

US troops on the march to Buffalo, New York State, with their camp followers.
American version of a Thomas Rowlandson caricature of British troops and their women.

headed back to Chippawa, where Street's Creek was being used as an entry point for supplies from Buffalo. During these days of maneuver, the British maintained contact with their enemy to learn his intentions.

By mid-morning on Monday, July 25, Lieutenant-Colonel Thomas Pearson's roving light troops had discovered the whereabouts of Jacob Brown's army. The Americans were camped on both sides of the Chippawa River: the 2nd and 3rd Brigades along the Niagara; the 1st Brigade on the south side of the river. Pearson posted his command—the Glengarry Light Infantry Regiment, Canadian infantry and cavalry militia, elements of the 19th Light Dragoons, three artillery pieces, and Norton's Indians—in total 1,200 men—around the junction of the Portage Road and Lundy's Lane, two and a half miles north of Chippawa. In the meantime, Drummond, who that day came from York to meet Riall, decided to concentrate all his forces at Lundy's Lane. He surmised it would be the perfect site from which to protect Forts George and Niagara, counter an American thrust at Burlington Heights, or attack Brown at Chippawa. Orders went out to Lieutenant-Colonel Joseph Morrison and his 800 regulars, plus Indians and an artillery detachment, nearby, to move to Lundy's Lane, arriving there at 6:00pm. The brigade of Colonel Hercules Scott, at Twelve Mile Creek, containing 1,500 regulars and 250 militia infantry, was also directed to head for Lundy's Lane.

As Drummond gathered his forces north of the American camp, Jacob Brown received disturbing reports. The first was of a British column moving from Fort Niagara down the American side of the Niagara River threatening Brown's main supply center at Schlosser. This was the case, but the British turned back before reaching that place. The second report stated that there was an enemy force above Chippawa. Brown ordered Winfield Scott's command to march north toward Queenston to investigate. This, Brown hoped, would abort any enemy move on Schlosser. Scott's 1,100 infantry, 70 dragoons and Towson's artillery marched at 5:00pm.

Around 7:00pm the head of Scott's column, marching on the Portage Road, spotted the British arrayed in battle formation on a low, flat hill. The hill was a

Virginian Brigadier-General Winfield Scott had natural leadership abilities. Drill, discipline, and motivation were the essence of Scott's training regime for his American soldiers.

sandy ridge running east to west for a mile, and was a half-mile wide. Fifty feet above the surrounding area, it sloped gradually to the south and west, but more steeply to the north and east. Lundy's Lane, a sunken, tree and fence-lined road, ran across its entire length. On its eastern margin was the Portage Road; on its western edge, a track ran south to Skinner's Farm a mile away. The height commanded a cleared area of farmland crossed by fences that extended to a chestnut wood 750 yards further south. East of the Portage Road, as well as to the north and west of the hill, were scattered fields and woods. The slopes of the ridge were clear of trees. About 250 yards west of Portage Road was a log meeting house and cemetery that crowned the hill. To the southeast and below the graveyard, on the slope stood an orchard and a family residence referred to in battle accounts as the "white house." Along the orchard, 300 yards in front of the hill, was a track connecting Portage Road with the path to Skinner's Farm.

Drummond placed his command thus: Captain James Maclachlan's five artillery pieces, and the Royal Marine Congreve Rocket detachment at the cemetery; to the rear of the artillery and in the center of the line was the regular infantry of the 89th Foot; to their right were three companies of the 1st Foot; holding the left flank on the Portage Road stood the Light Company of the 41st; light troops of the 8th Foot and some Incorporated Militia held the wooded extreme left between the Portage Road and the Niagara River

Gorge; on the west flank were stationed the dark green uniformed Glengarry Light Infantry, elements of the four Lincoln and one York militia regiments, and Norton's 500 Indians; and at the junction of the Portage Road and Lundy's Lane the blue-clad troop of the 19th Light Dragoons. The British line of 1,600 men resembled a concave curve with the hill at its center and its ends advanced.

Upon seeing the British position, Winfield Scott first considered retreating but then decided to take the bolder course of standing fast, giving the impression "upon the enemy that the whole American reserve was at hand and would soon assault his flanks." Scott then ordered his regiments to form line to the left of the Portage Road: the 9th on the left, the 11th in the center, and the 22nd on the right. Towson's three cannon went into battery on the road. As the brigade moved to deploy into line, the British artillery started to play among the Americans. According to 11th US Regiment drummer Jarvis Hanks, the enemy fire, "rattled around me" cutting "the branches of trees . . . splintered the [fence] rails." The cannonade caused parts of the 22nd and 11th Regiments to panic and break for the rear. Most of these men were quickly rallied and returned to the ranks.

Once formed, the American infantry started firing at the only targets they could see—the enemy guns on the hill, and the British 1st Foot on the US left. The rest of Drummond's force was positioned on the reverse slope of the ridge out of American view. While the Yankee muskets were too far away for their fire to be effective, the British artillery was

Brigadier-General Scott leads his men forward at the battle of Chippawa.

not. Relentlessly firing at the stationary enemy infantry, the British gunners did good execuvtion at a range of 600 yards. According to Lieutenant Samuel Brady, 22nd US Regiment, "We were completely cut up, more than half the officers and men being wounded." Towson's three pieces could not counter the opposing artillery, since his guns, although within range, could not be elevated enough to hit the British cannon.

After 45 minutes of this punishing artillery fire—of which a British officer later wrote that American "Dread seemed to forbid his advance, and Shame to retrain his flight"—Scott ordered his 1st Brigade to attack. It moved only 100 yards before stopping, presenting its left flank to the Glengarries, militia and Indians posted on the British right. The British moved to assail the American flank while some of the 1st Foot moved to the front of the hill to support this attack. Responding to the danger, the left-most companies of the US 11th wheeled back to face the Canadians. Both sides then exchanged fire, but as dusk approached neither made a move to advance.

If Drummond had made a "bold and gallant forward movement at once with his whole force and the bayonet," according to General Ripley's later reflections, it would have settled "in fifteen minutes" the fate of the 1st Brigade. This was the opinion of the remaining officers of the rapidly disintegrating unit. Drummond failed to advance because he felt that he was facing Brown's entire Left Division, a force he knew to be twice the number of his own.

Drummond was also distracted by the twilight attack made on his left by Major Thomas S. Jesup's 25th US Infantry, which had traveled north and then veered east, crashing into that British flank. The Americans drove the Canadian militia and British regulars west of the Portage Road and forced Drummond to face part of the 89th Foot to the east along with the rallied militia and 8th Foot contingent of his left wing. During Jesup's advance, the 25th captured a number of prisoners including General Riall, who had been wounded in the arm. But the Major, hearing that Scott's force had been beaten, retired south down the Portage Road. As he marched, he was met by reinforcements Jacob Brown had sent.

At 7:30pm, Brown at Chippawa heard cannon fire and assumed Scott was heavily engaged. Ripley's men, with Brown at their head, moved to Scott's assistance, while Porter's unit was put on alert. At the same time, the brigade of Colonel Hercules Scott was rushing to reinforce Drummond at Lundy's Lane. As this new force approached the battlefield at 9:00pm, after a 20-mile forced march, Drummond pulled the troops of both his right and center back to their original locations.

Brown reached the battlefield at 9:00pm and directed Ripley to march through the chestnut woods where "the enemy fire was very heavy," according to Ripley's aide, Captain William McDonald, and "fell about us in great quantities." Ripley's Brigade formed east of the Portage Road to the Skinner tract with the 23rd Regiment on the right, the 21st in the center, where it was ordered to assault the hill, while the 1st Regiment made a demonstration on the American left. When directed by Brown to move against the height, the commander of the 21st, Colonel James Miller replied, "I'll try, Sir!" But at that moment Lieutenant Colonel Roger C. Nicholas exceeded his orders and attacked the hill with his

1st US Regiment, and he was met by a hail of British cannon fire and forced to retreat to the base of the slope.

Nicholas's effort allowed Miller's regiment to move up the southeast side of the hill without encountering the British artillery fire directed at the 1st US. At 100 feet from the enemy cannon, the Americans let loose a volley that cut down many of the British gunners. A bayonet charge followed, which delivered the British ordnance into American hands. Drummond, who was close to the scene, ordered the 89th behind the British artillery line to recover the captured guns. The regiment entered the cemetery and exchanged musket fire with the Americans at 40 yards distance. The American did not budge, but after 20 minutes of intense musketry, the 89th pulled back. Sergeant Cummins of the 8th Foot mistakenly reasoned that the Yankees did not crumble under the British fire because they were "well fortified with whiskey [which] made them stand longer than ever they did." During this firefight, Drummond helped steady the 89th Foot until he was hit by a musket ball that entered his right ear and lodged in his neck. After two further failed attempts to charge and save their cannon, the British defenders retreated down the north slope of the ridge, leaving their guns in Miller's possession.

Over on the American right, the 23rd Regiment had gone up the Portage Road to assault the enemy gun position from the west. After encountering an ambush, which threw the unit into disarray, it finally ascended the hill.

Miller's charge at the battle of Lundy's Lane, July 25, 1814. Much of the fighting took place at night.

At 9:30pm, the 1st and 23rd US Regiments joined Miller's 21st on the formerly British-occupied eminence. Porter's 3rd Brigade, only 300 in number, arrived and was placed on the left—west of the 1st Regiment—angling down the slope. There its line was extended south by the 19th US Infantry from Scott's brigade. The rest of 2nd Brigade was aligned along Lundy's Lane, supported by three artillery companies. Meanwhile, Drummond had reformed his army a few hundred yards north of his original position, his force stretching from the Portage Road to west of the Skinner tract.

At 11:30pm the British initiated a final counterattack against their old position. At this time, Winfield Scott made his last attack of the day from the middle of the American line on Lundy's Lane, but was forced back, retiring to the west and out of the battle.

Soon after, Jacob Brown, near the position of the 1st US, was struck by a musket ball in the right thigh, then he was hit in his left side, but did not leave the field. Nearing Porter's men, the British 103rd, parts of the 1st, the Incorporated Militia, and 41st Regiments, advanced and traded volleys with 3rd Brigade. Porter charged his foe, and with the help of the 1st US Regiment, pushed the Redcoats back. On the American far right, after the British closed to within effective musket range, a 30-minute duel commenced with the US 25th, which Jesup, having sustained four wounds in the fight, remembered as a "contest now more obstinate than in any of the previous attacks of the enemy . . . but our fire was so well directed and so destructive that the enemy was again compelled to retire."

In the center of the British line, the attack of the 89th Battalion on the right, the 8th in the middle, and elements of the 1st Battalion on the left, was directed at the captured British guns, and according to General Ripley this last effort "compelled the whole line [of the US 1st and 25th Regiments] to recoil, and it was with unexampled difficulty that it was rallied." A fierce struggle took place among the artillery pieces, only resolved when first the British flank units pulled back, followed by their center forces, leaving the cannon and the hill crest to the American Left Division.

The Battle of Lundy's Lane, after five hours of heavy fighting, was over—and the Americans had held their own. Brown, before leaving the field to tend to his wounds, ordered Ripley to withdraw the badly mauled division back to Chippawa where it arrived on the 26th. Without enough horses, Ripley did not attempt to haul away the captured British guns. Instead, they were recovered by Drummond next day when he reoccupied his hilltop position. He not only reclaimed all but one of his lost artillery pieces, but two American cannon as well! Brown ordered Ripley on July 26 to go back to Lundy's Lane and bring off the captured guns, but as the latter made his way to the battlefield with 1,500 men, he was informed that a superior number of British were waiting for him there and he immediately returned to Chippawa. The bloodiest battle of the war cost Brown 173 dead, 571 wounded and 117 missing; Drummond suffered 84 killed, 559 wounded, 235 missing or captured.

✦ ✦ ✦

Having suffered severe casualties, his men exhausted, and fearful of an enemy attack, Ripley, commanding the Left Division while Brown was recuperating from his wounds, decided to retreat to Fort Erie. The incapacitated General Brown let his subordinate carry out this withdrawal. At 11:00pm on the 26th, the Left Division limped into the fort. On August 2, moving from Queenston, Drummond arrived six miles from Fort Erie. Even before the British neared his position, Ripley had begged Brown to allow him to move the division across the Niagara to the American side. Brown scornfully rejected Ripley's proposal. Ripley then set to work, strengthening the post's defenses by adding to the original small stone structure a series of earthworks connecting it with Lake Erie, and extending it 800 yards south to Snake Hill, a sand mound made into a formidable artillery battery. The place was then surrounded by a wide ditch and dense abatis. Beyond the fort, the area was cleared up to 400 yards, allowing the installation's 18 heavy guns a clear field of fire. This was supplemented on the fort's north side by the guns at Black Rock, New York, as well as three US Navy Schooners anchored in the lake.

To breach the American position, Drummond prepared a battery sporting five heavy guns sited near the lake north of the fort. His bombardment began on August 13 and continued through the next day. But the British cannon, 1,100 yards from the fort, were 400 yards too far away to injure the defenses. One British observer stated that not "one shot in ten reached the rampart at all," and the ones which did reach the stone building, "rebounded from its sides as innocuous as tennis balls."

On the 15th, Drummond planned to storm the fort. His plan called for Indians to make a feint to draw off some of the garrison between Snake Hill and the stone fort. A little later, a southern column of 1,500 from the De Watteville and 8th Regiments would assault Snake Hill. After that point was taken, from the north 300 men of the 104th Regiment would hit the stone fort itself, while another force to its left, composed of 700 men from the 103rd Regiment, took the entrenchments running from the fort to the lake. A small reserve was to follow and clean out any resistance remaining.

Advancing in the dark, the attackers were repulsed at all points. Some managed to gain a small entry into the stone fort but could not penetrate the defenses further, and were decimated by an explosion in the stone bastion from ammunition stored on a lower floor. The effort cost the British 2,500-man storming force 57 dead, 309 wounded, and 905 missing. The defenders lost 62 soldiers.

The siege continued but the British were hampered by the appearance of the American lake fleet, which blockaded the mouth of the Niagara, cutting off food and weapons to the British besiegers. Two more batteries were constructed nearer the fort by early September, and 1,200 new troops arrived to bolster Drummond's force, but on the 16th he decided to lift the siege.

Next day, as the Redcoats started to dismantle their siege lines, the Americans, under orders from Brown, sallied out from the fort. The plan called for Porter to move from Snake Hill and take the British in the flank. Soon after, James Miller would attack directly from the American center. The initial Yankee attack, made in the rain, quickly captured two of the enemy batteries. Counterattacked by the now alerted Canadians and regulars,

Miller and Porter's forces could not reach the last enemy artillery position. Ripley led a reserve force to their rescue but got lost and was wounded. The attackers retreated back to the fort after losing 79 dead, 216 wounded (including Porter) and 216 missing; Drummond lost 115 killed, 183 injured and 316 missing.

After decamping from Fort Erie, Drummond moved to the Chippawa River, arriving there on September 24. He was followed by the Americans, under General Izard who, outranking Brown, was put in charge of the Niagara sector in mid-October. Unable to goad Drummond into a fight, Izard returned the Left Division to the United States on October 24. Marking a finale to Jacob Brown's offensive, on November 5 Izard removed all American troops from Canada, blew up the fortified works at Fort Erie, and ended the Niagara Campaign of 1814—the hardest fought operation of the war.

Elite British Riflemen. Figure standing is from the 60th Regiment—originally the Royal American Regiment recruited to defend the American colonies in the mid-18th century—an extra battalion was raised for the War of 1812. Figure kneeling is from the 95th Rifles that fought at New Orleans.

CHAPTER NINE

Britain Invades America

⊰••••⊱

LIEUTENANT JAMES SCOTT, AIDE TO BRITISH REAR ADMIRAL GEORGE COCKBURN, noted in his post-war recollections that his boss had long "fixed an eye of particular interest upon Washington [and that] every measure he adopted was more or less remotely connected, conceived and carried into execution" with a view to capturing the American capital. Toward that end, on July 17, 1814 he wrote to London outlining his plan. He suggested a landing at Benedict, Maryland, followed by the rapid seizure of Washington, DC, and then taking Baltimore and Annapolis.

The British blueprint to conduct more vigorous offensive operations along the US Eastern seaboard had been in the works well before Cockburn formulated his scheme, or the war against Napoleon had ended in Europe. These proposals were merely accelerated after the French Emperor's first abdication in April 1814. Thousands of British regulars from the Duke of Wellington's Peninsular Army had been transported from Europe across the Atlantic to Canada during the spring and summer of that year in preparation for increased land and naval pressure on the Americans.

To ensure this goal, the Admiralty transferred command of the North American Station from Admiral Sir John B. Warren to the more offensive minded 56-year-old Vice Admiral Sir Alexander Inglis Cochrane. A captain by the end of the American Revolutionary War, from 1790 to 1813 he served as commander of individual warships and squadrons in the English Channel, the Mediterranean, Western Atlantic and West Indies before formally replacing Warren in April 1814. Like Cockburn, Cochrane was eager to capture the enemy capital and prophesied that the town could be "either destroyed or laid under contribution." By mid-July, Cockburn's naval force operating in the Chesapeake Bay was

British Royal Artillerymen clad in blue uniforms rather than the usual scarlet.
Contemporary illustration by Charles Hamilton Smith.

enlarged by the appearance of additional men-of-war and a battalion of Royal Marines. News also arrived that Cochrane was sailing from Bermuda with thousands more British troops to join him.

While the British threat to America's coastline and capital grew, the Madison administration slowly recognized the danger. On July 1, 1814, President Madison suggested that a force of 3,000 armed men be placed between Washington and the Chesapeake Bay, 50 miles to the east, and that another 10,000 militiamen be put on alert in the District of Columbia and the neighboring states. Next day, to facilitate the President's order, the 10th Military District was formed, encompassing the 200-mile-long Chesapeake Bay, Maryland, the District of Columbia, and northern Virginia between the Rappahannock and Potomac Rivers. Brigadier-General William Winder was given command of this new military zone. That spring, Winder had been released from British custody after his capture at the battle of Stoney Creek the year before. His appointment, over the objection of Secretary of War Armstrong, was purely political since his uncle, Governor of Maryland, would provide the bulk of the military force to defend Washington. Winder's qualifications as a soldier were summed up by Lieutenant-Colonel William Duane, Army Inspector General's Department, when he wrote that Winder "knew no more of military matters than his horse, and I am satisfied that he could not put a company in motion after two years experience."

Over the next six weeks, Winder made no moves to fortify his charge or concoct a plan for its defense. His inertia was aided by Armstrong's refusal to concede any threat to Washington. This conceit translated into not letting available militia take the field unless there was an imminent threat of an assault on the capital. To those who foresaw an enemy descent on Washington, Armstrong berated them by proclaiming, "But they certainly will not come here [Washington]. What the devil, will they do here? No! No! Baltimore is the place, Sir. That is of so much more consequence."

The British strategic goal in the Chesapeake was based upon the premise of creating distractions that would aid British efforts on the Canadian front. The directive from the British Secretary of State for War and the Colonies stated that the troops with Cochrane's fleet were "not to engage in any extended operations at a distance from the coast," nor try to occupy any place permanently. Tactically, the commanders on the spot elected to go with Cockburn's plan, composed of two parts: diversionary naval raids up the Potomac River and the Eastern Shore to draw defenders away from the capital, and a march on Washington.

With a view to masking their designs on the capital, the Royal Navy chased down the Row Galley squadron of American Commodore Joshua Barney, a Revolutionary War hero, whose flimsy sail and oared barges hovered in the Patuxent River (which flowed south and east into Chesapeake Bay), constituting the only American naval defense in the area. Conveniently, this preliminary operation brought the British within a day or two's march from Washington.

On August 18, Cochrane's fleet of 46 men-of-war and transports entered Patuxent River, disgorging men and material at the small river port town of Benedict, 25 miles up

British Field Officer of the Royal Engineers.

from its mouth. Next day, the British ground force commander, Major-General Robert Ross, organized his troops into three brigades, one each under Colonel William Thornton, and Lieutenant-Colonels Arthur Brooke and William Patterson. His force included the 4th, 44th, 21st and 85th Light Foot Regiments, as well as 600 Royal Marines, a contingent of sailors, three artillery pieces, and Congreve rockets—a total force of 4,500 men.

Major-General Ross, born in Dublin in 1766, embarked on a military career with the British Army in 1789, rising to the rank of Colonel in 1808 after seeing service in Holland, Egypt and Spain. From 1812–14, he fought under Wellington in the Iberian Peninsula and was made Major-General. He was seriously wounded at the battle of Orthez. While recovering from his injuries, he was named commander of the expeditionary force assigned to Admiral Cochrane's fleet in the war against the United States. Courageous, cautious, deferential, a strict disciplinarian, and loved by his men, Ross was a soldier's soldier.

On August 20, Ross set out west on foot with Cockburn's small boats on the river paralleling the army's march. The target was Barney's little flotilla at Pig Point. Cockburn's marines and sailors reached there on August 22, only to see the 17 vessels of Barney's squadron blown up by the Americans. Barney's 400 flotilla men and five cannon then marched to join the gathering Washington defenders. That day, Ross' command reached Upper Marlboro, Maryland, less than 20 miles from Washington, after covering 39 miles from Benedict in sweltering summer heat, but against no opposition. By the 23rd, Admiral Cochrane, who was becoming uneasy about the distance between the fleet and Ross' army, ordered the General to return to Benedict; but Cockburn convinced Ross to continue on to Washington.

Meanwhile, Winder had since the 18th called on all available troops to muster at Wood Yard, 12 miles east of the District of Columbia; the militia from the Baltimore region were to rendezvous at Bladensburg, Maryland, ten miles east of the capital. On the 22nd, the 10th Military District commander concentrated his forces at Battalion Old Fields (modern Forestville, Maryland), eight miles from the British then laying at Upper Marlboro, and the same distance from Washington. On the morning of August 23, the British, leaving their marines behind, started the 12-mile trek to Bladensburg. In response, Winder pulled back to Washington from his Battalion Old Fields site.

At noon on the 24th, the red-clad column sighted US troops beyond Bladensburg. They were formed on the west bank of the Anacostia River to deny the 120-foot-long bridge over the waterway to the British. The American position to the east was bordered by the river's marshy bank. Low ground sloped slightly higher to the west. The Old Bladensburg-Georgetown Road, and the Washington Post Road met 75 yards west of the bridge to form a single avenue. One mile southwest of the bridge was a ravine crossed by Turncliff's Bridge. A 600-yard-long north to south ridge, cut by several gullies, was further west. The entire area was mostly open fields, offering little concealment, dissected by fences.

Defending the west side of the river, just across from Bladensburg, was Brigadier-General Tobias Stansbury's 11th Maryland Militia Brigade. By not occupying Bladensburg, he failed to avail his men of the trenches dug there by the Americans the week before. In addition to his infantry, he set up an artillery battery on the road covering the bridge. To the right of the guns were Pinkney's Rifle Battalion; to the left-rear were a few infantry militia companies. Behind this screen, he placed the 1st, 2nd and 5th Maryland Militia Regiments, with a battery and 380 dragoons to their left. Further back on the ridge, west of Turncliff's Bridge, Winder established a third line made up of Brigadier-General Walter Smith's 1st Columbian Brigade (DC militia), on the left of the Washington Post Road. Barney's seamen, some US Marines and five artillery pieces took station to the right of the DC militia astride the road, while militia from Annapolis held a small height on Barney's right. Stansbury had ordered the span over the river destroyed but that was not done. Furthermore, the second American line was spread out too widely to effectively support the first line.

At 1:00pm, Thornton's Light Brigade, having arrived at Bladensburg ahead of the rest of the British army, was given permission by Ross to attack. This was a risky decision, since in case of a setback the unit would be unsupported. Nevertheless, the 85th Regiment and one light company of the 4th Regiment charged through Bladensburg and over the bridge, six abreast. Sergeant David Brown, 21st Foot, recalled that "the bridge was crossed under a heavy fire of musketry and artillery, with tremendous effect for at the first discharge almost an entire company was swept down." Captain James Knox of the 85th, seeing the casualties mounting from his outfit, felt that "by the time the action is over, the devil is in it if I am not either a walking major or a dead captain." Regardless of the losses, the British kept crossing. As American militiaman Henry Fulford wrote, the Redcoats "took no notice of [their losses] . . . the instant a part of a platoon was cut down, it was filled up by the men in the rear." Once on the west bank, and Pinckney's riflemen had been dispersed, the British light troops deployed in open order and rushed Stansbury's second line, only to be pushed back to the river by a counter-charge from the 1st and 2nd Maryland Regiments.

In response, Ross threw in his recently arrived 4th and 44th Regiments, ordering their brigade commander Arthur Brooke to threaten both enemy flanks after he crossed the river. He then rushed off to personally encourage the men of the 85th Regiment. Once the 4th crossed the water, they struck the American right, while the 44th did the same on the other flank. All the while the Marylanders of the second line were being pummeled by Congreve rocket fire. The new enemy push drove Ragan's 1st Maryland Militia Regiment from the field and endangered both wings of the 5th Maryland Regiment, causing it, and the adjoining cavalry, to flee down the Washington Post Road in great disorder.

With the entire American defense line dissolving in retreat, the British shifted their assault straight down the road at the new anchor of the American line—Commodore Barney, his naval artillery, and some US Marines. But "Wellington's Invincibles" were halted, according to the Commodore, who ordered an 18-pounder to be fired "which completely cleared the road." Barney's cannon barked twice more at the advancing enemy who were either killed or thrown back. Avoiding the sting of the American 18-pounders on the road, the British hit Barney's right flank, receiving two ragged volleys from the Maryland militia units guarding there, before the Americans fled before the point of British bayonets.

British troops march into the American capital and set fire to it on August 24, 1814.

After just having his horse shot from under him, Ross ordered a thrust at Barney's left against Colonel George B. Magruder's nervous 1st DC Militia Regiment, scattering them. Seeing this, a panicky Winder directed the infantry supporting Barney's naval guns to fall a short way back. They did, but failed to stop until they were off the battlefield. Ross took advantage of this error and sent his infantry directly at the now exposed enemy artillery's right. As the British closed on the gun position, American navy and marine officers shouted to their men, "Board 'em, board 'em"—the only close quarter combat order they knew. As the position was overrun, Barney was wounded in the hip by a musket ball and captured, while his men spiked the guns and fought their way to safety. The other artillery unit fighting alongside Barney, Major George Peter's Battery, also escaped.

The battle of Bladensburg cost the ill-trained American army of 6–7,000 men, no more than 40 killed and 60 wounded, with 120 captured, along with ten artillery pieces. Ross lost 64 dead, 185 wounded, and 107 deserted or captured. It was a contest marked by poor generalship on both sides, each commander attacking piecemeal, risking defeat in detail.

By the 25th, the American fugitives from the battle had either gone home, like Smith's 1st Columbian Militia, or were rallying, like the remnants of Barney's boatmen and newly arriving Maryland and Virginia militia, at Rockville, Maryland. The British did not pursue the Americans for more than a mile after the fight—the 95-degree heat and the fatiguing pre-battle march prevented them from doing so. However, at 6:00pm, Ross and Cockburn, escorted by Patterson's men, marched to Washington, which was entered by the Admiral and General with a 200-man patrol at 9:00pm on the 24th. While near the Robert Sewell House, looking for someone to negotiate the surrender and ransom of the city, Ross' party was fired on, losing one killed and three wounded. Ross fell from his mortally injured steed, but was unhurt. Immediately, the building from which Ross' party received the shots was stormed, but the perpetrator got away. The house was then set on fire since it had been used for hostile purposes. Ross then proceeded to set up a bivouac on Capitol Hill.

British troops march into the American capital and set fire to it on August 24, 1814.

✦ ✦ ✦

The city Ross and Cockburn entered had been largely abandoned by its population of 8,000, many of its citizens preferring to hide in the woods rather than remain in town under British occupation. Elbridge Gerry, Jr. sarcastically wrote to his wife from the capital, days after it was occupied by Ross, saying that many tried to leave the city on the enemy's approach "but were out run by the militia." The days leading up to the battle of Bladensburg saw the evacuation of government documents to Leesburg, Virginia, while official records and legal tender went to Frederick, Maryland. Some war material from the Washington Navy Yard had also been removed. President Madison and a small party wandered about Rockville after Bladensburg, while Winder headed for Baltimore, and Armstrong arrived at Frederick.

Once in control of the American capital, Cockburn urged Ross to burn it to the ground in retaliation for the destruction of York in Upper Canada in 1813. Ross compromised by ordering the destruction of all the public buildings only. To Lt. George R. Gleig, 85th Light Infantry, a veteran of the Peninsular War, the resulting firestorm so impressed him that he wrote: "Except for the burning of St. Sebastian [in Spain], I do not recollect to have witnessed at any period of my life a scene more striking or sublime." The US Senate and House of Representatives chambers in the Capitol Building were burned by Ross's Quartermaster General, Lieutenant George De Lacy Evans, and Lieutenant James Pratt of the Navy. A number of junior officers were outraged by the order—a Captain Smith writing later that "I had no objection to burn[ing] arsenals, dockyards etc, but we were horrified at the order to burn the elegant Houses of Parliament." On the lower floor of the House, Cockburn found Madison's copy of the receipts and expenditures of the US Government for 1810. He kept it as a memento of his triumph. Soon the rising wind blew fiery embers onto the shingle roof of the Library of Congress, dooming that edifice.

Determined to obliterate the US Supreme Court building, British arsonists piled furniture on the main floor and set it alight, but the building's brick vaulting held firm and kept the fire at bay. As the flames spread through the city, Ross accepted lodgings in the house of Dr. James Ewell. Ross and Cockburn then took 100 soldiers and sailors to the White House. At 10:30pm, the intruders found that the staff had fled and that the main dining area had been prepared to serve 40 guests. Hungry and parched, Ross and his men helped themselves to the feast. He then had his Chief Engineer, Captain Thomas Blanchard, burn the structure down. As the interior of the President's home was consumed by fire, Cockburn removed from it a chair cushion as a souvenir. An eyewitness reported how the White House was quickly engulfed in flames: "The spectators stood in awful silence, the city was alight and the heavens reddened with the blaze." Dr. Ewell also commented on the President's house burning, horrified by the flames that burst through the windows "and mounting far above its summits, with a noise like thunder, filled all the saddened night with gloom." However, the great sandstone walls withstood the heat and remained standing. The brick US Treasury building on the east side of the White House was then burnt. To Mordecai Booth, a US Navy Department clerk, who saw the capital in flames from near

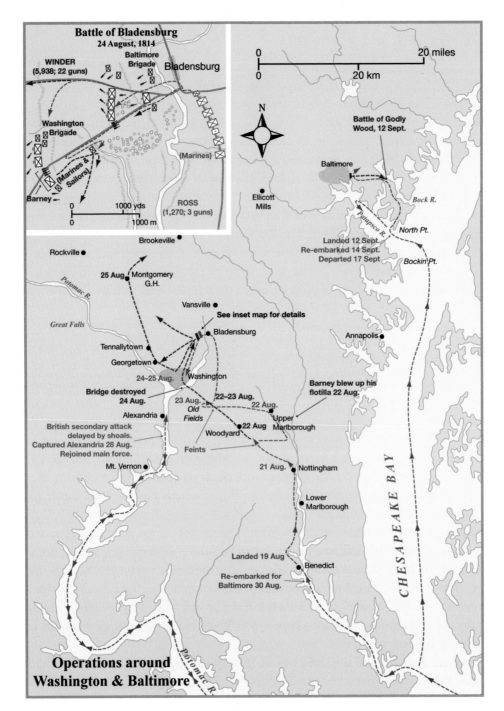

Battle of Bladensburg
24 August, 1814

WINDER
(5,938; 22 guns)

Baltimore
Brigade

Bladensburg

Washington
Brigade

(Marines)

(Marines &
Sailors)

Barney

1000 yds

1000 m

ROSS
(1,270; 3 guns)

N

0   20 miles

0   20 km

Battle of Godly
Wood, 12 Sept.

Baltimore

Bock R.

Ellicott
Mills

North Pt.

Landed 12 Sept.
Re-embarked 14 Sept.
Departed 17 Sept

Bockin Pt.

Brookeville

Rockville

25 Aug. Montgomery
G.H.

Vansville

See inset map for details

Great Falls

Bladensburg

Annapolis

Tennallytown

Georgetown

24–25 Aug.   Washington

Bridge destroyed
24 Aug.

23 Aug.
Old
Fields

22–23 Aug.

22 Aug.

Barney blew up his
flotilla 22 Aug.

Upper
Marlborough

Alexandria

Woodyard

22 Aug

British secondary attack
delayed by shoals.
Captured Alexandria 28 Aug.
Rejoined main force.

Feints

Mt. Vernon

21 Aug. Nottingham

Lower
Marlborough

Landed 19 Aug

Benedict

Re-embarked for
Baltimore 30 Aug.

C H E S A P E A K E   B A Y

Potomac R.

Potomac R.

Patapsco R.

**Operations around
Washington & Baltimore**

the Washington Navy Yard, it was "A sight so repugnant . . . so dishonorable, so degrading to the American character, and at the same time so awful."

Anticipating its capture, the Americans had destroyed the Washington Navy Yard, including the warships *Essex* and *Argus*. The sight moved Mary Hunter, a city resident, to comment: "You never saw a drawing room so brilliantly lighted as the whole city was that night. Few thought of going to bed—they spent the night gazing on the fires and lamenting the disgrace."

At midnight, Cockburn, after prowling around the city, came across and wrecked the office of the *National Intelligencer* newspaper, and was only prevented from having it fired by the pleas of some locals fearing the proposed burning would spread to their homes. A late night rainfall dampened down most of the blazes set by the British and saved great parts of the town. Next day, amid the continuing flames and petty plundering by officers, as if to assuage their guilt, a British enlisted man was apprehended for looting and shot.

Washington's destruction continued on the 25th with Ross completing the demolition of the Navy Yard, the burning of the State and War Department offices, and the Long Bridge across the Potomac River. The US Patent office was spared. Not so the Green Leaf's Point Arsenal, which due to an accident blew sky high the buildings, ammunition and 75 British soldiers carrying out its destruction. Writing home, an officer who witnessed the catastrophe stated that the carnage at the arsenal was "a thousand times more distressing than the loss we met with in the field of Bladensburg."

A severe thunderstorm touched down that day, uprooting trees and tearing off rooftops, adding to the fiery chaos on the ground. Men, horses, even cannon, were tossed about by strong winds. Finally at 8:00pm, fearing an American attack, Ross secretly led his men out of the capital to rejoin the balance of his force at Bladensburg while Washington continued to burn and glow in the dark as the British departed. One American in Washington at the time believed that Ross had reason to be worried, writing that, "At this moment a legion of troops [such] as Colonel H [Henry "Light Horse'] Lee, could have entered Washington and have routed Ross, Cockburn, and as many of the incendiaries, drunk on the night of the conflagration, as they pleased to select." That evening the entire British army marched out of Bladensburg, arriving at Benedict on the 29th. Two days later, it embarked on Cochrane's ships.

The British public received the news of the sack of America's capital as an example of their army and navy's military prowess, and payback for American destructive acts to private property in Canada. For many US citizens, however, the events at Washington stirred national pride and increased their support for the war and the Madison administration. It also revealed the magnitude of the British threat to many who had previously felt the conflict was not their concern. What happened at Washington determined many to protect their communities.

As the British made their way out of the capital city, two last casualties of the campaign were identified. Secretary of War Armstrong, strongly blamed for the defeat at Bladensburg and subsequent capture of Washington, resigned his post on September 4, handing over the job to James Monroe. William Winder, equally excoriated for what many were calling the "Bladensburg Races"—after the way the American defenders fled the battle area in great numbers—went on leave after the troops in Baltimore refused to serve under him. He left the army in 1815.

✦ ✦ ✦

As reprinted in the *Niles Weekly Register* of September 24, 1814, London newspapers in mid- year prophesied that the British troops currently pouring into North America would "in all probability" target Washington, Philadelphia or Baltimore, "but more particularly Baltimore." This prosperous city—at the time the third largest in the United States—sat at the head of the Patapsco River in the northern reaches of the Chesapeake Bay and was most bothersome to the British war effort. Over 250 licensed privateers operated out of the town against British merchant shipping, and she was a hotbed of pro-war sentiment. The destruction of the large amounts of naval stores held there would not only hurt the American war effort, but would also bring in profits from prize money for her conquerors.

Admiral Cochrane and General Ross embraced the idea of attacking Baltimore, since their schedule demanded preparation for a descent on the Gulf of Mexico. Furthermore, activities by Cochrane's amphibious force closer to New York, rather than continuing in Chesapeake Bay, would better relieve the pressure on Canada demanded by his government. However, just as he did before the march on Washington, Ross was convinced by Cockburn that Baltimore must be assaulted, with both of them then persuading Cochrane to follow that course.

Baltimore was in a strong position to resist an enemy attack. The port city had wealth to finance an effective defense, and a strong leader in Samuel Smith to direct it. Smith, a veteran of the Revolutionary War, a militia general prior to the conflict of 1812, a merchant and US Congressman as well as a Maryland State Senator, had the prestige and wisdom to unite the city's populace and coordinate the town's protection. By early September he had fielded 15,000 militiamen, and strengthened Baltimore's defenses at Fort McHenry, on a peninsula that projected into the harbor.

Smith correctly believed the British attack would come from the east, landing near North Point, in conjunction with a naval thrust at Baltimore Harbor. He therefore constructed a defense line covering that area on Hampstead Hill, consisting of more than a mile-long stretch of earthworks and gun emplacements, anchored by Fort McHenry.

On September 11, Cochrane's fleet moved into the Patapsco River. Upon learning this, Smith ordered 55-year-old Revolutionary War veteran Brigadier-General John Stricker's 3,000-strong 3rd Maryland Militia Brigade to move seven miles east of Baltimore to the area on Long Log Lane, below Trappe Road. Here a blocking position was set up where the land was less than a mile wide, bordered on the north by Bread and Cheese Creek, and to the south by Bear Creek. In front of the American line, which ran along a tree-lined fence, were open fields with little cover, over which the enemy would have to advance. As the night progressed, more troops joined Stricker. As he developed his land position, hulks were sunk in Baltimore's harbor channel, with armed barges behind them acting as floating gun batteries. This prevented enemy ships from dashing into the port and delivering overwhelming firepower on the town or Fort McHenry.

The next day, three miles from Stricker's encampment, the British landed at North Point over 4,000 men and eight pieces of artillery. Information from three captured American scouts mentioned a force of 20,000 ready to defend Baltimore. To this, assuming the number represented untrained militia, Ross replied, "I don't care if it rains militia." He was

*Rear-Admiral George Cockburn relishes his moment of victory by standing on the
Speaker's Chair in the US House of Representatives.*

convinced that he had a clear road to his objective until he reached Hampstead Hill. Before
the General left to join his advance guard, he was asked if he would be returning that
evening for supper. Ross reputedly answered, "I'll set up tonight in Baltimore or in Hell."

The American defense at Long Log Lane was composed of the 5th Maryland Militia
Regiment to the south of the road, its right connecting with some riflemen and cavalry,
which extended the entire American right to Bear Creek; an artillery battery on the road
itself; and the 27th Maryland Militia Regiment to the left of the road, placing its left flank
on Bread and Cheese Creek. Stricker formed a second line 300 yards behind the first, with
the 51st Maryland Regiment to the right and 39th Maryland Regiment to the left. A half a
mile further back on Long Log Road was stationed the 6th Maryland Militia Regiment.

At 1:00pm, the British advance bumped into American pickets a half-mile from the
American main line. A brisk skirmish ensued. Ross and Cockburn had been riding to the
front when the firing began. Half an hour later, intending to bring up his main body, Ross

turned in his saddle and said, "I'll bring up the column." At that moment, he was struck through the right arm and right chest by a combination of buckshot and ball, falling from his mount mortally wounded and dying two hours later. It appears the General had been shot at by three militiamen picking peaches in front of the American line.

As Ross was carried to the rear, Colonel Arthur Brooke of the 44th moved to the front of the British column and took command—"an officer of decided personal courage but better calculated to lead a battalion, than guide an army." He directed artillery to engage the enemy cannon, and placed his light troops to cover his entire front while an infantry line was formed. This was made up of a naval detachment positioned on the road just above Bear Creek; behind them was the 21st Foot, and then another Royal Marine contingent. To the right of the sailors and marines on the front line stood the 85th Light Foot, and to its right the 44th Foot. Around 2:30pm, Brooke sent his 4th Regiment by way of a concealed path to turn the American left flank. Stricker countered this move by moving parts of his 39th Regiment and two cannon to his left, followed by the 51st Regiment.

The British 4th reached its jump off position and charged, followed by the rest of the British line. The Maryland 51st panicked, as well as a battalion of the neighboring 39th Regiment, with both fleeing the field. But the remainder of Stricker's line held firm. Twenty yards from the American line, Brooke ordered his men to halt, fire a volley and then close with the bayonet. Lieutenant Gleig recalled that during this charge, "The Americans instantly opened a tremendous fire of grape upon us but reserved their musketry until we should get closer." The opposing sides came together for a fierce ten-minute, close-quarter encounter, before the American line collapsed and retreated back to the position of the 6th Maryland Regiment a half-mile to the west.

Admiral Cockburn's aide, Lieutenant Scott, thought the enemy retreat was "a second edition of the Bladensburg Races." Agreeing with Scott, Gleig concluded that "I never in my life saw a more complete rout. Horsemen, Infantry, Guns and all mixed together running like a flock of sheep, and our fellows knocking them over in dozens." Regardless of those British officers' opinions, Stricker's men moved off the battlefield in relatively good order, and after forming line further west, were prepared to receive any following enemy. But Brooke did not pursue. He thought he was vastly outnumbered, and his men were worn out by the heat and the combat of the day. The fight, called the battle of North Point, cost the Americans 24 killed, 139 wounded and 50 captured. The British suffered 39 killed, including Ross, 251 wounded, and 50 missing.

On September 13, the British neared Hampstead Hill with its 11,000 defenders supported by 100 cannon. While an aborted attempt to turn the enemy line from the north by Brooke was going on, at 3:00pm Admiral Cochrane launched his attack on Fort McHenry, after which he planned to thrust into Baltimore Harbor and unhinge the fortified Hampstead line for the army. Half an hour later, three Royal Navy frigates, brigs, and tenders anchored five miles from the fort, while five bomb vessels—each capable of hurling 200-pound mortar shells at a rate of one every five minutes at 4,200 yards—and the rocket ship *Erebus* approached within two and a half miles.

Fort McHenry was commanded by Major George Armistead, a regular US Army officer. Under him 1,000 infantry and gunners manned the post with its 36 heavy cannon. The British opened fire on the fort out of range of the defenders' ordnance, which had a maximum range of 2,000 yards. Armistead later reported that even though he could not return fire since the enemy was out of range, and that "we were left exposed and thus inactive, not a man shrunk from the conflict." As the enemy barrage rained down on the installation, one of the American 24-pounders was disabled, then a British shell crashed into the fort's main powder magazine—but fortunately proved to be a dud. Witnessing the intense bombardment of the fort, the Reverend John Baxley scribbled in his diary that "Such a terrible roar of cannon and mortars I never heard before."

After eight solid hours of pounding the enemy position, and the American return fire slackening, Cochrane sent in three rocket vessels and the bomb ship to finish the job. They were met by heavy fire, pulled back out of range, and resumed firing. The shooting continued all night. A British landing party during the evening was put on shore to take the fort from the rear. Noticed by the defenders, it was driven back to their landing boats. At 7:00am on the 14th, after refusing to support Brooke's attack on Baltimore's land defenses—because he would have to bring his ships within range of Fort McHenry's guns—the Admiral halted the entire operation and recalled Brooke and his troops back to the fleet. Fort McHenry had been on the receiving end of 1,500 shells fired at it, 400 landing within the structure. The defenders lost four killed and 24 wounded.

It was at this time, too, that a civilian onlooker, Francis Scott Key, was so inspired to see the American fort withstanding the attack, that he composed a poem, later put to music, which became the US national anthem, "The Star Spangled Banner."

After the British troops retreated from Baltimore with no enemy interference, they embarked on their transports on the 15th. For two days, the British fleet remained off North Point until it returned to the Patuxent River. Cochrane would not renew his assault on Baltimore since he had to prepare for a campaign in the Gulf of Mexico. His "invasion" of US territory at Baltimore had suffered a setback. And another such British effort, much further north, had already experienced a more serious defeat—one that would greatly contribute to the war's end.

✦ ✦ ✦

The order, dated June 3, 1814, arrived that July marked "Secret" and was titled "Reinforcements allotted for North America and the operations contemplated for the employment of them." It contained instructions from the British Government to Sir George Prevost, informing him that 10,000 British soldiers were being sent to Canada before the year's end to be used "to obtain, if possible ultimate security to His Majesty's possessions in North America." It went on to give several suggestions for future operations. One that particularly stood out was the injunction that "Should there be any advance position on that part of our frontier which extends towards Lake Champlain, the occupation of which would materially tend to the security of the province, you will if you deem it expedient expel the

Enemy from it, and occupy it." With this directive in hand, and large numbers of rein-forcements on their way, Prevost determined to strike at the enemy army at Plattsburg, New York, by land and water. After breaking the Americans there, he could winter on the edge of Lake Champlain—100 miles south of the Canadian border—and in the spring of 1815 threaten New York City. With peace talks about to start at Ghent, Belgium, a bold move such as this might end the war on British terms, and give Canada a new and more secure frontier.

Contemporary cartoon depicting King George III "In Mud to his Ears" in the War of 1812, caught between a Kentucky rifleman and a Louisiana Creole.

Putting his plan into effect, Prevost started to concentrate his army at Chambly, 20 miles south of Montreal, and 20 miles north of the American border. Of the 30,000 troops he would eventually command, he created a 9,700-man division of three infantry brigades as the initial spearhead for his invasion of the United States. His field force would also have his old Canadian Fencibles and Voltiguer units, 40 field guns, a number of siege pieces, 536 artillerymen, 172 Congreve rocketeers, and 340 dismounted troopers from the 19th Light Dragoons. Commanding his three infantry brigades were three Major-Generals chosen by the Duke of Wellington, all new to Canada. However, over them was placed the uninspiring Baron de Rottenburg.

Since the operation Prevost envisioned needed support from the navy to take control of Lake Champlain, and thus protect the army's supply route and flank, the Lake Champlain squadron was hurriedly strengthened. Its leader, Captain George Downie, led a force of brigs and sloops, 11 gunboats and HMS *Confiance*, a 37-gun frigate with long range 24-pounders—a third bigger than any American vessel, and the largest ship to sail on Lake Champlain up to that time. But all this took time, since the commander of all British naval forces on the Great Lakes, James Yeo, absorbed with operations on Lake Ontario, allotted little means to the Lake Champlain base at Isle-aux-Noix with which to build up its squadron. Furthermore, he and Prevost were not on good terms, which made military and naval cooperation on the lakes a dicey proposition throughout the entire war.

Opposing Prevost in the Champlain area was Major General George Izard, who by the end of August 1814 had 4,500 men at Chazy (12 miles north of Plattsburg) and Champlain, and another 600 working on fortifications at Plattsburg and Cumberland Head, just northeast of Plattsburg Bay. Situated on the west shore of Lake Champlain, Clinton County, New York, the town of Plattsburg was a natural gateway from Canada into the United States via the Richelieu River–Lake Champlain axis. During July, Izard concentrated his entire force around Chazy and Champlain under his second in command, Brigadier-General Macomb.

Alexander Macomb was a 32-year-old from Detroit, Michigan, but raised in New York City. A militia junior officer in the late 1790s, he entered the US Regular Army in 1801, becoming part of the elite Engineer Corps and rising to Colonel of the 3rd US Artillery Regiment by the eve of the War of 1812. After performing capably under Dearborn and Wilkinson during their campaigns of 1813, and the latter's early 1814 foray into Canada, he was promoted Brigadier-General. He briefly succeeded Wilkinson as commander of the Right Division at Plattsburg in early 1814. After Macomb was replaced there by Izard, he spent the entire summer drilling his brigade.

The impending British invasion by Prevost was such a well-kept secret that Izard was unaware of the menace through most of the summer. As a result, in July he asked the Secretary of War to be transferred to the Niagara Front, where active operations had been going on. His request was granted, but then learning of the enemy threat in early August he asked that he be allowed to remain at Plattsburg. Armstrong denied Izard's new motion, and the General left Plattsburg with 4,000 troops on August 27. Macomb was left in charge of the Plattsburg area with 3,000 US regulars and 1,500 militiamen.

"Everything is in a state of disorganization," Macomb lamented in a letter after taking charge at Plattsburg, "works unfinished and a garrison of a few efficient men and a sick list of one thousand." Things got worse when requests for the turnout of New York and Vermont militia moved at a glacial pace, if at all. Then, on August 31, a British infantry brigade crossed the border and camped on the north bank of the Great Chazy River—the rest of Prevost's army followed the next day. Macomb was urged by members of his staff to retreat to the south, but the General declined, determined to rely on his fortifications around Plattsburg, and he gathered his entire force to do just that.

The works Macomb planned to defend were three in number, and formed a straight line across the narrow peninsula that separated the Saranac River from Lake Champlain: Fort Brown stood just above the Saranac; Fort Moreau at the center of the peninsula; Fort Scott near the banks of Lake Champlain. Each was a large earthen emplacement fairly secure from the north, but more vulnerable from the south if they could be attacked from the rear. Two blockhouses, one covering the lower bridge over the Saranac, and the other where that river enters the lake, were also built and manned as outposts.

On September 1, Master Commandant Thomas Macdonough brought his squadron, with 820 men manning his ships, into Plattsburg Bay in preparation to meet the British naval force supporting Prevost's invasion. The young American naval officer was born in Delaware, joining the US Navy at age 17. After participating in the First Barbary War, he was made a lieutenant, then in October 1812 put in charge of the American Lake Champlain squadron, performing yeoman service throughout the war.

Macdonough picked Plattsburg Bay because the winds would be blowing against the British when they tried to enter it. Also, the confined space there would be to his advantage, due his superior number of short-range carronades. His ships had 35 carronades to Downie's 27, whereas the British had the advantage in longer-range pieces, 48 to the American's 35. Once in the bay, he formed his ships in line running northeast to southeast: the 20-gun brig *Eagle* at the north end, next the 26-gun *Saratoga*, then the 17-gun schooner *Ticonderoga*, and the seven-gun sloop *Preble*. Each ship had hawsers—cables—attached to its bow anchor and extending to the stern, and could be turned by hauling on the port or starboard hawser. Ten gunboats, with a total of 16 cannon, were placed in groups of two or three 40 yards west of the ships.

On September 4, the British army camped at the village of Chazy. The next day, the army moved toward Plattsburg in two parallel columns. On the 6th, the British right column passed East Beekmantown and engaged in a day-long skirmish with 700 New York militiamen supported by two artillery pieces, Macdonough's gunboats, and 250 regulars under Major John Wool, who returned to duty soon after his wounding at the Battle of Queenston in 1812. In these brawls, the Redcoats lost 103 men, the Americans 45. Wool wrote long after the war about his rearguard actions against the British 3rd Foot Regiment along the Beekmantown Road. He recalled that though he was heavily outnumbered and hotly pressed, and his horse was shot from under him, his command "disputed every foot of ground until it arrived on the right bank of the Saranac in the village of Plattsburg." He also claimed that he received no support from any militia until the close of the day. Regardless of Wool's successful rearguard actions, that same day Prevost's columns joined up and occupied Plattsburg, its 3,000 inhabitants having fled the borough. But he chose not to cross the Saranac River in the face of American forces on the south bank.

For the next several days, the British, while awaiting the arrival of their fleet, probed the bridges and fords over the river. They set up four artillery emplacements with the 16 heavy cannon, howitzers, and mortars that accompanied the army from Canada. The first salvos from theses were fired on the American works on the 11th. That day, Downie's squadron, with a total of 917 men, sailed from its base at Isle-aux-Noix, its final departure delayed due to the work that needed to be completed on HMS *Confiance*. With her sailed the 16-gun brig *Linnet*, the 11-gun sloops *Chub* and *Finch*, and 11 gunboats sporting guns.

On September 11, Downie sailed into Plattsburg Bay, hampered by the wind as he tacked northward into the bay. The battle, starting at 9:00am, quickly broke down into two segments: *Eagle, Saratoga* and seven gunboats against *Confiance, Linnet* and *Chub* at the north end of the line; *Ticonderoga, Preble* and three gunboats facing *Finch* and four gunboats—the other eight British gunboats never getting into battle. Fifteen minutes into the contest, *Chub* had her sails and rigging so damaged that she drifted out of control through the American line and surrendered. On the other end of the line, *Finch* was so badly hurt by *Ticonderoga* and *Preble* that she lost control and struck a reef on Grab Island and surrendered. Meanwhile, the American *Preble* ran aground, leaving *Ticonderoga* to finish the battle fighting four British gunboats, which repeatedly without success tried to board her.

On the opposite end of the American line, *Eagle* was pounded by *Linnet* and *Confiance*. *Eagle* then retired behind *Saratoga*, allowing the two British ships to devote their full attention to the latter. During this phase of the battle, Macdonough was wounded and the

U.S. Capitol after burning by the British. Courtesy of the Library of Congress

American cartoon accusing British of paying American Indians for scalps. This was not true; the British paid the Indians to bring in prisoners alive. Courtesy of the Library of Congress

British commander, Downie, killed. *Saratoga* turned on her hawsers to bring her port guns to bear on *Confiance*. The British vessel attempted the same maneuver to bring her undamaged starboard side into action, but failed. As she tried to swing about, Asa Fitch, the purser on *Saratoga*, recalled how his ship fired her undamaged battery stuffed to the muzzles with handspikes at *Confiance*, with the result that, "Where it had been black with men the moment before, scarcely one man could now be seen." *Confiance*, battered and unable to fire, surrendered at 11:00am. Twenty minutes later, after being pounded by *Saratoga*, the *Linnet* struck her colors. By this time most of the British gunboats had fled the scene.

On the day after the fight, Macdonough sent a message to Secretary of the Navy William Jones, stating, "The Almighty has been pleased to grant us a signal victory on Lake Champlain in the capture of one Frigate, one brig and two sloops of war of the enemy." The battle cost the Americans 52 killed and 58 wounded; the British 54 dead, 116 injured. At day's end, both fleets lay shattered in the bay, not a sail of either functioning, and the Americans barely saving their main prizes, the floundering *Confiance* and *Linnet*.

It had been a fierce encounter, with HMS *Confiance* receiving 105 shots to her hull and almost sinking, while USS *Saratoga* sustained 55 hits. Julius Hubbell of Chazy remembered that "The firing was terrific, fairly shaking the ground, and so rapid that it seemed to be one continuous roar, intermingled with spiteful flashing from the mouths of the guns, and dense clouds of smoke soon hung over the two fleets." After viewing the wrecked *Confiance*, he found her "absolutely torn to pieces" with mutilated bodies everywhere on her deck.

As the naval battle raged, Prevost ordered his 1st and 3rd Infantry Brigades of 4,000 men to assail the ford at Pike's Cantonment. After the British column became lost, they arrived at the crossing an hour later and rushed over the ford, dispersing 400 American militia guarding it, then waited for the rest of the army to pass to the south bank. While doing so, the British were under American artillery fire, with Captain James H Wood, Royal Artillery, being almost hit by a round shot that "stupefied me for some minutes and an inch or two closer would have made me shorter by the head." At 3:00pm an order arrived, calling for a retreat from Plattsburg since the Royal Navy had lost control of Lake Champlain in that day's fight. Major-General Frederick P Robinson, in charge of the assault force, summed up the feelings of the entire British army after receiving the order to withdraw, saying, "Never was there anything like the disappointment expressed in every countenance. The advance was within shot, and full view of the Redoubts [the three American forts guarding Plattsburg area], and in one hour they must have been ours. We retired under two six-pounders posted on our side of the ford in as much silent discontent as was ever exhibited."

Prevost's army hastily withdrew to the area around Montreal, closing down campaigning on the Lake Champlain Front for the rest of the war. His advance on Plattsburg was the first and last major offensive he conducted. Aside from the sacking of Washington, the only unqualified British achievement of 1814 was the easy occupation of the eastern third, including 100 miles of coastline, of Maine. That incursion was designed to serve as an all-British route from Quebec to Halifax. When peace was made, most of the area was returned to the United States.

Peace talks convened in August at Ghent, Belgium, with all eyes turned toward the US-Canadian frontier in anticipation of events there, which would determine the shape of the final settlement. The battle of Plattsburg vindicated that attention, but action in the Gulf Borderland also contributed its share in the making of peace.

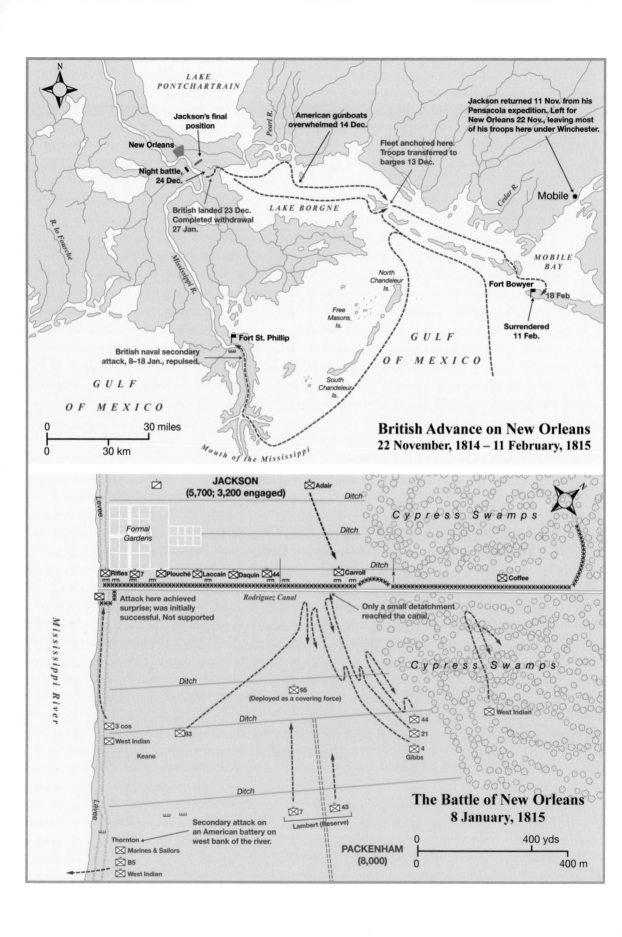

British Advance on New Orleans
22 November, 1814 – 11 February, 1815

LAKE PONTCHARTRAIN

Jackson's final position

New Orleans

Night battle, 24 Dec.

British landed 23 Dec. Completed withdrawal 27 Jan.

Pearl R.

American gunboats overwhelmed 14 Dec.

Fleet anchored here. Troops transferred to barges 13 Dec.

LAKE BORGNE

Jackson returned 11 Nov. from his Pensacola expedition. Left for New Orleans 22 Nov., leaving most of his troops here under Winchester.

Cedar R.

Mobile

MOBILE BAY

Fort Bowyer

18 Feb.

Surrendered 11 Feb.

R. Jo Fourche

Mississippi R.

North Chandeleur Is.

Free Masons Is.

Fort St. Phillip

British naval secondary attack, 8–18 Jan., repulsed.

GULF OF MEXICO

GULF OF MEXICO

South Chandeleur Is.

0   30 miles

0   30 km

Mouth of the Mississippi

The Battle of New Orleans
8 January, 1815

JACKSON (5,700; 3,200 engaged)

Adair

Ditch

Cypress Swamps

Formal Gardens

Ditch

Rifles 7 Plouché Laccain Daquin 44 Carroll Coffee

Ditch

Levee

Rodriguez Canal

Attack here achieved surprise; was initially successful. Not supported

Only a small detachment reached the canal.

Mississippi River

Ditch

95 (Deployed as a covering force)

Cypress Swamps

West Indian

Ditch

3 cos

93

44

21

West Indian

Keane

4 Gibbs

Ditch

7 43

Lambert (Reserve)

Secondary attack on an American battery on west bank of the river.

Thornton

Marines & Sailors

B5

West Indian

PACKENHAM (8,000)

0   400 yds

0   400 m

CHAPTER TEN

War in the South and the Battle of New Orleans

=⟫⟫⟪⟪=

IN THE SOUTH, "THE FIRE OF THE MILITIA WAS UP" AGAINST THE CREEKS, WROTE Andrew Jackson to Governor Willie Blount of Tennessee in June 1812. "They burn for revenge," he continued, "and now is the time to give the Creeks the fatal blow." Jackson's comments were in response to murders of whites earlier in the year by Creek Indians, whose confederacy spanned western Georgia and eastern Alabama. Those responsible were called "Red Sticks—from their practice of carrying wands painted red denoting war— and since 1811, encouraged by Tecumseh, were resisting the Americans. Many were Upper Creeks living in central Alabama, who rejected the white man's ways and his encroachment on Indian lands. In contrast, the Lower Creeks, residing in western Georgia and eastern Alabama, adopted white culture, extensively intermarried with whites, and made accommodations with the US government. By the spring of 1813, Creek depredations against whites were numerous, and the Creek nation was near civil war, pitting pro-white Lower Creeks against the Red Sticks.

The Americans believed that the British and Spanish furnished aid to the Creeks prior to the start of the War of 1812. The British did intend to support the Indians in the event of conflict with the United States, but did not take action to incite the Creeks to war before 1814. The Spanish favored an attack by the Indians on the US as the only way to defend Spain's weakly held East and West Florida; however, neither Spain nor Britain proved willing to fully supply the Creeks with arms until after their defeat at Horseshoe Bend in 1814. As a result, during the struggle between the United States and the Red Sticks, the latter could never supply and arm more than 2,500 fighters at any one time, with only one in three warriors possessing any type of firearm.

Seeking weapons and ammunition to carry on their fight with the pro-white Creeks, 300 Red Sticks, led by Peter McQueen, an influential half-breed among the tribe, visited the Spanish at Pensacola, Florida, in early summer 1813. They received powder and lead but no guns. On his way back to western Alabama, McQueen's party was attacked by180 undisciplined militia from the Mobile area under Colonel James Caller, who wanted to forestall an Indian war by capturing the munitions before they could be distributed.

Near Burnt Corn Creek, 80 miles north of Pensacola, on July 27, 1813, Caller's men attacked the Creek pack train and its dozen drivers. One hundred Creeks, who had crossed the water before the pack train approached, counterattacked, catching the militia by surprise, regaining their supplies, and scattering the Americans. This first fight between US military forces and Creeks during the War of 1812 claimed five dead and ten wounded Americans, versus two killed and five wounded Red Sticks.

Buoyed by his success at Burnt Corn Creek, and wishing to destroy a white settlement, McQueen targeted isolated Fort Mims on the east bank of the Alabama River, 35 miles north of Mobile in Mississippi Territory (the future states of Mississippi and Alabama). The fort, the strongest in the Territory, housed 553 whites, mixed bloods, friendly Indians and Negro slaves—all the types despised by the Red Sticks as representative of pro-white Creek society. Joining McQueen was William Weatherford, born in 1780, the

Massacre of white settlers at Fort Mims by Creek Red Sticks warriors in August, 1813.

Portrait of a Creek chief in 1820s, son of a Scots father and native mother. Many mixed-blood warriors fought on both sides during the Creek War.

child of a Scottish trader and a Creek woman, who was a Creek chieftain and wealthy planter. Weatherford, known as Red Eagle during the war, later claimed he was forced to join the Red Sticks since his family was being held hostage by them. He became the Creeks' most capable military leader.

Defending Fort Mims was Major Daniel Beasely, a lawyer with little military experience, and 240 militiamen and armed settlers. This force would have been enough to protect the post, except Beasely took no defensive precautions to thwart an attack. At noon on August 30, 750 Creeks assaulted the fort while the garrison was at lunch. The Indians rushed the place, a few surging through the fort's open main gate, which could not be closed due to a sand mound that had accumulated against it. Beasely was killed as he tried to shut the jammed portal. Meanwhile, other Indians wrestled the fort's rifle loopholes from the control of the defenders, making a defense of the fort's walls impossible.

The defenders fought on inside the fort, but the Indians set it on fire and cut them down "like beeves in the slaughter pen of the butcher's." Forty whites and mixed bloods escaped the inferno; 275 whites, mixed bloods and friendly Indians were either killed or taken captive. The murdered suffered awful deaths. Captain Kennedy, head of the burial party, reported that "Indians, negroes, white men, women, and children lay in one promiscuous mass." All were scalped and the females of every age were butchered. He went on to record, "The main building was burned to ashes, which were filled with dead bones." As the massacre took place, Weatherford claimed he had implored that the women and children be spared, but his pleas were ignored. The attackers lost over 200 killed and wounded.

After Fort Mims, the Red Sticks had no real plan of action other than Weatherford's strategy of creating a series of strongpoints throughout the Creek territory from which the warriors could strike the enemy as he approached.

✦   ✦   ✦

The American reaction to Fort Mims called for the invasion of the Creek confederacy by four armies from different directions, combining at the junction of the Coosa and Tallapoosa Rivers, where they formed the Alabama River. During their march to the rendezvous point, the several columns were to engage Red Stick forces, burn enemy villages, destroy Indian crops, and build and garrison stockades the entire length of the routes of advance. The projected three-month campaign to subdue the Creeks turned into ten due to chronic shortage of supplies and the constant turnover of militia.

The first operations against the Red Sticks occurred along the Alabama River when General Ferdinand L. Claiborne, head of the Mississippi Territorial Militia, set out from Fort Stephens in western Alabama on October 12, 1813, to clear the area of the Alabama and Tombigbee rivers. He went on with his 1,200 men to capture Weatherford's hometown of Holy Ground, containing 200 houses, on December 23. Less than 50 Indians under Weatherford opposed Claiborne, and after a sharp fight he retreated with a loss of 33 Red Sticks killed, while the Americans suffered one dead and 20 wounded.

Claiborne built a number of forts on the Alabama River, which cut communication between the Creeks and the Spanish at Pensacola, and cleared the lower part of the river of the enemy. In January 1814, he had to discharge his militia, and for the rest of the war the American troops on the Alabama River were too few to undertake anything but minor raids. But control of the Alabama made possible the transit of supplies, which sustained the operations of the main forces thrown at the Red Sticks, allowing them to remain in Creek country.

The force under Brigadier-General John Floyd moved west from Georgia to the confluence of the Coosa and Tallapoosa Rivers to join with the army moving south from Tennessee under Andrew Jackson. Floyd's command of 1,500 men (including 400 friendly Indians) advanced 60 miles from the Chattahoochee River to the hostile town of Autosse, located on the south bank of the Tallapoosa River, 20 miles above its junction with the Coosa. On November 29, he formed his force into two columns: the right bordering Calabee Creek, while the left one surrounded Autosse and an adjacent village. Severe fighting erupted at dawn, the Indians being driven back to the woods behind the towns. Their lines

French Pirate Jean Lafitte offers his services to Governor Claiborne (middle) and General Jackson (right) during the battle for New Orleans—and subsequently received a pardon for his efforts providing men for its defense.

were finally broken after Floyd bombarded Autosse with his artillery, followed by a bayonet charge. Both villages were burned, but most of the Red Sticks escaped after losing 200 killed and scores more wounded. The white army lost 11 killed and 54 wounded, including Floyd, and many allied Indians. Floyd wrote after the battle that so many Indian dead were found in heaps near the creek that the "river near the shore was crimson with their blood."

Floyd then retreated to the east shore of the Chattahoochee, his search and destroy mission completed, but hobbled by lack of provisions and the pending expiration of most of his militiamen's term of service. Floyd took the field again in mid-January, moving 41 miles west of the Chattahoochee where he erected Fort Hull. He had 1,100 militia and 600 natives under his command.

Hoping to defeat the invaders before Fort Hull was completed, the Red Sticks struck the American encampment at night on January 27, 1814. The camp was formed in two separate squares. Floyd recalled the Indian assault: "They stole upon the sentinels, fired upon them, and with great impetuosity rushed upon our line; in 20 minutes the action became general. . . . The enemy rushed within 30 yards of the [two pieces of] artillery." The initial Indian onslaught drove the soldiers from part of their camp, and the severest part of the battle centered around the cannon.

Andrew Jackson with the Tennessee forces. Courtesy of the Library of Congress

Floyd lost 21 whites killed and 128 wounded, as well as five friendly Creeks killed and 15 wounded. The Red Stick total came to 49 killed and wounded. Although repulsed, the hostiles had badly mauled the Americans and carried out their most skillful attack of the war. In mid-February, Floyd took what remained of his militia back to Georgia, leaving Fort Hull garrisoned. It became a collection point for supplies intended for Jackson's army when it reached the Coosa and Tallapoosa Rivers.

✦ ✦ ✦

As part of the concentration against the Creeks, General Andrew Jackson's 2,500-strong militia force left Tennessee for Ten Islands on the upper reaches of the Coosa River on October 25, 1813. Like the other American forces engaged against the Creeks, Jackson was chronically short of food. On November 2, he ordered Brigadier-General John Coffee's 900 Tennessee Volunteers and a party of allied Indians to attack the large Creek town of Tallasahatchee, 13 miles from present day Jacksonville, Alabama.

Coffee reached Tallasahatchee early next morning and placed his command, split into two columns, in a concealed circular formation around the town. The right column consisted of volunteer cavalrymen, the left of mounted riflemen. Two companies of horsemen were sent out in the open to draw out the enemy, who, seeing the exposed mounted detachment, rushed out to attack them. These retreated, pursued by the Creeks. After coming up to Coffee's hidden right, and receiving a strong volley of fire from the mounted troopers, the Red Sticks were halted in their tracks. The cavalry then charged, followed by the American lefthand column. Soon the Creeks were enclosed in a deadly circle and were slain as they fell back among the town's houses. Red Stick losses were 186 killed, with 84 women and children taken prisoner. Coffee lost five killed and 41 wounded. The town was demolished and the expedition rejoined Jackson's main force at its new base called Fort Strother near Ten Islands.

On November 7, Jackson heard that the friendly Creek village of Talladega, 30 miles from Fort Strother and defended by 160 warriors, was under siege by 1,100 Red Sticks. Gathering 1,200 infantry and 800 horsemen, Jackson made for Talladega. At 4:00am on the 8th, he formed three infantry columns abreast, with cavalry behind the left and right columns, and an advance guard of horsemen. The army took on a crescent shape with cavalry on the right and mounted infantry on the left wing. The object was to encircle the enemy once contact was made.

As at Tallasahatchee, a small American mounted advance element drew out the besieging Creeks, who attacked them, forcing the riders to retreat. The oncoming Red Sticks unnerved a militia brigade that started to crumble before them until mounted infantry from the reserve plugged the gap and repulsed the advancing enemy. The next 15 minutes witnessed continuous firing between the Red Sticks and the American infantry as Jackson's mounted wings closed the circle on the Creeks. Realizing the trap they were in, the Indians escaped through a hole in the American line, Jackson pursuing the fugitives a few miles. Over 290 Creeks were killed, while Jackson lost 15 killed and 85 wounded.

Lack of supplies prevented the US commander from continuing his offensive operations, and the next month saw his men, on the verge of starvation, demand release from service due to expired enlistment terms. A number of times the men started home to Tennessee until stopped by Jackson and his remaining loyal troops.

After much of his army disintegrated in December 1813, Jackson gathered a force of 800 infantry, 130 mounted men and 100 Indians. Raiding south of the Coosa River from Fort Strother, he beat the Red Sticks in two minor engagements at Emuckfau and Enitachopco. During February and March he organized a new army of 2,000 infantry, including the well-trained 39th US Infantry Regiment, 700 cavalry, 600 Indians and two pieces of artillery. On March 24, he set off from Ten Islands to attack a large Creek encampment on the Tallapoosa River.

Andrew Jackson's headquarters at the Macarty house.

At the Tallapoosa, 1,000 Creeks had constructed a breastwork across the neck of a bend in the river. The barrier—ranging five to eight feet high—had a double row of loopholes that allowed enfilade fire on any attacking force. Approaching his objective on the 27th, Jackson sent his mounted troops and most of his Indians, under Coffee, two miles below the Creek breastworks in order to surround the bend on the far bank and cut off any escape in that direction. During the battle, Coffee's men swam the river, took the Creek village, and laid down fire into the backs of the Red Sticks defending the breastwork against Jackson's main attack. The occupation of an island in the river opposite the western end of the Creek fortifications by Coffee deprived the Red Sticks of a place of refuge.

In the meantime, the American army was positioned in front of the Indian works, with the artillery 80 yards away from the nearest part of the enemy position. At 10:30am, the soldiers commenced a two-hour artillery bombardment that had little effect. Musket fire was also directed at the barrier when targets presented themselves.

Fearing that Coffee's isolated men would be overwhelmed, Jackson ordered a direct charge on the breastwork. The regulars and militia surged forward and a fierce fight ensued. Major Lemuel Montgomery, 39th US Regiment, joined by Lieutenant Sam Houston, future hero and president of Texas, mounted the top of the parapet. Montgomery was shot dead while Houston, hit in the thigh by an arrow, engaged the warriors in hand-to-hand combat. The Indians broke but continued to fight desperately, since their planned retreat across the river had been thwarted by Coffee's men. The battle then became a series of mopping up operations. One group of Red Sticks gained shelter under a bluff near the river. Houston stormed the position with a few others, receiving two more wounds for his trouble. Fire was used to flush the fugitives out and they were gunned down as they tried to escape the flames.

The battle of Tohopeka, better known as Horseshoe Bend, cost Jackson's army 26 killed and 106 wounded, most of them from the US 39th. Jackson's Cherokee allies lost 18 killed and 36 wounded, while his friendly Creeks sustained five dead and 11 wounded. Red Stick casualties were 557 killed at or near the barricade, while 300 more were shot down in the river trying to flee. This was attested to by militia officer Major Alexander McCulloch, who wrote: "The Tallapoosa might truly be called the River of Blood for the water was so stained that at 10 at night it was very perceptibly bloody, so much so it could not be used." For all practical purposes, this battle ended the Creek War, as the remaining hostiles either surrendered or fled to Florida. William Weatherford gave himself up, and Jackson, out of respect for his opponent's bravery and ability, allowed him to go free. On August 9, 1814, Jackson signed the Treaty of Fort Jackson, concluding peace with the Creeks and forcing them to cede 23 million acres—half their homeland—to the United States and move further west.

✦ ✦ ✦

"I hasten to communicate to you," wrote Secretary of War James Monroe to Andrew Jackson on October 21, 1814, "the directions of the President, that you should at present take no measures which would involve this Government in a contest with Spain." In other words, the Madison administration denied the General's requests during that October to allow him to capture the Spanish held city of Pensacola. But Jackson, as of May 28 the new commander of the Seventh Military District—encompassing Louisiana, Tennessee, the Mississippi Territory and West Florida—had no fear about a war with Spain if it meant US possession of Pensacola.

On August 22 Jackson moved his district headquarters to Mobile and, in complete disregard of his government's wishes, prepared to capture Pensacola, insisting that its capture was vital for the defense of Mobile and New Orleans against the British. Neglecting the defenses of New Orleans, "Old Hickory" led a 4,500-man army to Pensacola.

On November 7, 1814, Jackson camped his army on the west side of the town, facing the place's main defenses: Fort St. Michael, on a hill 400 yards from the town's west edge, supported by several blockhouses, and Fort Barrancas, located on the west shore near the entrance to Pensacola Bay. The Spanish garrison was made up of 500 infantry, some artillery, and an unknown number of British troops. Jackson determined to surprise them by attacking from the east.

To fix Spanish and British attention away from the real point of assault, Jackson sent 500 men to demonstrate against the town from the west. Meanwhile, at 9:00am, the General marched his main body in three columns on a circuitous route out of sight of Fort St. Michael to the east side of Pensacola, three miles distant. Once positioned, the Americans charged into the city: the column made up of regulars moving along Center Street; the men of the Tennessee volunteer force entering the street to their right; while the column made up of Choctaw warriors marched on the next street along the rear of the town in view of Fort St. Michael. Artillery attached to the attackers fell behind. The US regulars were met by three volleys of enemy artillery, and musket fire from a blockhouse and residences lining the street. Some cannon fire fell on the Americans from the British ships anchored in the bay. After a spirited charge by the Americans, all these obstacles were cleared, and a counterattack by Spanish troops from Fort St. Michael was easily repulsed. This was followed by the surrender of city. The entire action lasted less than half an hour.

Jackson's triumph cost seven killed and 11 wounded, in exchange for the deaths of 14 Spanish and six others hurt. Elated by the performance of his soldiers, he remarked to Governor Blount of Tennessee, "The steady firmness of my troops has drawn a just respect from our enemies." On the 8th, as the Americans contemplated how to take Fort Barrancas, the British saved them the trouble by evacuating the 200-man Spanish garrison and blowing up the installation before sailing away. They relocated 150 miles to the east to the mouth of the Apalachicola River from which they continued to supply the Red Sticks and harass Georgia and West Florida for the rest of the war.

The capture of Pensacola was a significant triumph in the Gulf Coast Campaign. It deprived the British of a key base from which to conduct activities in the area, and reduced their options for future operations in the Gulf. This came on the heels of a failed naval bombardment and amphibious assault on American-held Fort Bowyer, an earth and log structure at the head of Mobile Bay, on September 15. After trading short-range gunfire for two hours with the 160-man garrison and its 11 medium cannon, the British four-ship squadron had a 20-gun vessel sunk and a brig badly damaged. A 250-man British Marine and Indian party, with one artillery piece, gained the rear of the fort, but after being fired on by the defenders promptly withdrew. This small but important action cost the British 32 killed and 37 wounded, while the defenders lost four dead and five wounded. After the repulse at Mobile, followed by the fall of Pensacola, Admiral Cochrane concentrated all his plans for the Gulf campaign on a direct attack on New Orleans.

After taking Pensacola and now focusing on the importance of Mobile, because it "will be able to protect the pass from New Orleans, and prevent the enemy from cutting

Aerial view of battle of New Orleans showing British forces attacking the Line Jackson.

off our supplies," Jackson scattered his forces to forestall any threat to Mobile. One thousand horsemen were sent to the Apalachicola River to hunt down Redcoat detachments, Red Stick holdouts, and destroy this new enemy base. He strengthened the Mobile area, including Fort Bowyer, with three regular infantry regiments, and sent General John Coffee's 1,200 volunteer mounted riflemen to Baton Rouge. By the time Jackson reached New Orleans on December 2, the city was protected by only two under strength regular regiments and some militia.

The British had been considering an attack on New Orleans before the War of 1812 commenced. "Where the Americans are most vulnerable," wrote Admiral Cochrane in April of 1812, "is New Orleans and Virginia." In a June 20, 1814 letter, he outlined a plan to take the city with the help of Indian allies, after securing a base of operations at Mobile.

New Orleans, the wealthiest population center in the United States, situated 105 miles upstream from the mouth of the Mississippi River, was vital to the economy of the states of the South and Midwest since it served as the main entry and exit point for commercial trade in that part of the country. The British motive for seizing the place was to use it as a bargaining counter in any peace negotiations.

From the start, the operation to take New Orleans went forward in piecemeal fashion, altered by events, such as the denial to the British of the use of Pensacola or Mobile as a logistical base. Cochrane reported, "The attack made by the Americans upon Pensacola has in a great measure retarded this service [the British Gulf offensive]." Also, the large participation of Indians the British counted on never came about due to the Red Stick defeat at Horseshoe Bend. What kept the plan alive was that throughout the US Seventh Military District during the latter part of 1814, there were only some 3,000 regular troops scattered about the entire region. Local militiamen were the only other forces near the Gulf Coast.

New Orleans was a difficult target. Above the mouth of the Mississippi River, it is located on dry land but surrounded by marshes, swamps, shallow lakes and the river itself. Except for a few trails and boat channels, the marshes and swamps were impassable. Of the seven practical routes that the British Army could have used to approach New Orleans, Jackson was convinced they would come up the Mississippi River, or through Lake Pontchartrain. He therefore strengthened his defenses at those points. As for the other approaches, lack of manpower, weapons, and time to fortify them made him rely on detachments of local militia to block those avenues by felling trees and establishing a series of coastal outposts. This was done well except that Major General Jacques de Villere, of the Louisiana militia, failed to completely plug those channels of Bayou Bienvenue which extended from Lake Borgne into the General's own plantation close to the city.

By mid-December, the American force in New Orleans was meager, just 1,000 regulars from the 7th and 44th US Infantry, a few artillery companies, and 2,000 militia. Nearby were General John Coffee's 1,600 riders at Baton Rouge. A further 5,200 Tennessee and Kentucky volunteers were also marching to the city but were weeks away. Naval forces for the defense of the town consisted of six gunboats, a 12-gun schooner and a 16-gun sloop, all under the command of Commodore Daniel Patterson. Although small arms were in short supply, the navy yard at New Orleans contained a large number of heavy cannon that would play a vital role in the coming fight for the city.

From Jamaica, Admiral Cochrane's fleet entered Lake Borgne on December 13, 1814. With him were 7,500 British soldiers and marines under the command of Major-General John Keane. Facing him were five gunboats, carrying a total of 45 cannon, under the command of Lieutenant Thomas ap Catesby Jones. Next day, since the Americans were in water too shallow for the British fighting ships to reach them, 1,200 sailors and marines in 42 boats and barges—each carrying a chaser gun at its bow—rowed up the lake against the current to engage the US squadron. It took 36 hours to catch the enemy, but after a spirited two-hour fight, all the US vessels were captured. The British then made their initial landings at Pea Island. On the 23rd, a landing was made in Bayou Bienvenue, a stream 20 miles east of New Orleans. Because the Mississippi delta prevented the British ships from proceeding up the river, the landing of troops and supplies had to be conducted by boats after a 70-mile row upstream.

The lack of enough shallow draft craft was a serious obstacle to British success at

New Orleans, and placed a huge cost in time and manpower on the resupply effort. British Admiral Edward Codrington wrote about the problem, stating that "about 30 miles from where the frigates were, we assembled the whole army, but the labor of effecting this with our same means [the boats alone], and transporting the necessary ammunition and provisions, is beyond description."

After disembarking at Bayou Bienvenue with 1,800 men, Keane opted to await reinforcements instead of attacking New Orleans. He set up camp at General Villere's plantation, eight miles from the city. After learning of the enemy presence at Villere's homestead, Jackson gathered 2,131 Tennesseans under Coffee, local militia and US regulars, with two six-pounders, to engage Keane. The gunboat *Carolina* set sail to support the American land attack. The rest of Jackson's command, perhaps 3,000 men, was detailed to guard the area between New Orleans and Lake Pontchartrain, in case Keane's force was a diversion and the real enemy advance came through the Gentilly Road.

Under a full moon, the American army neared the British camp. It was then formed

Andrew Jackson directs the action at the battle of New Orleans. Painting by H. Charles McBarron.

American artillery pound British soldiers. Jackson portrayed on the right.

with the regulars on the right next to the river, artillery in the road, and Coffee's brigade with Colonel Thomas Hind's Mississippi Dragoons on the left. At 7:30pm, the *Carolina* moved past the British bivouac and fired her guns at the enemy campfires until 9:00pm. The Redcoats returned fire with three-pounder cannon and Congreve rockets. Neither side inflicted much damage on the other.

When the American ship opened up on the British, Coffee's men charged the enemy right, over ground crossed by ditches and fences, hoping to outflank it. The British were pushed back 300 yards, and then the 85th Light Regiment ran into Coffee's men and were thrown back by their accurate fire. In their turn, Coffee's Tennesseans fell back after his opponent rallied a new line behind an old abandoned levee, and arriving British reinforcements began to curl around Coffee's left. Along the main road, Jackson's infantry and artillery drove back the British advance posts, manned by the 95th Rifles, until British resistance stiffened and thick ground fog made control of the American units impossible. Lieutenant Gleig, 85th Light Regiment, summed up the hard nature of the action when he reported that British officers and men in small groups "fought hand to hand, bayonet to bayonet, and sabre to sabre." Captain John Cooke of the 43rd Light Regiment concurred with Glieg, saying that "since the invention of gunpowder, there is no instance of two opposing parties fighting so long muzzle to muzzle." To the left of the road, US regulars

General Jackson and his staff at the height of the battle. In the background, American troops capture a British standard.

of the 7th and 44th pressed the enemy back. In the American center, the force of the attack surprised the British. An anonymous Louisiana militiaman wrote "That they [the British] had no patrols, and appeared to be as happy and unconcerned as if encamped in Devonshire in England." But the militia units failed to keep up with their comrades on either wing and eventually were ordered to halt.

During the fight the American artillery was almost captured, saved only after "Old Hickory" ordered parts of the US 7th Regiment to their rescue. Fighting stopped at 9:00pm, with the American army retreating two miles back behind the Rodriguez Canal. For Keane, the cost of the first battle for New Orleans was 46 killed, 167 wounded and 64 captured. Jackson's army lost 24 killed, 115 injured and 74 prisoners. Surprised by the boldness of his opponent, and surmising that Jackson would not have attacked if he did not have a sizable force, Keane remained in place until the rest of his 6,500 troops joined him. For his part, Jackson planned to continue the fight the next day until he realized that large numbers of British reinforcements were arriving. Neither commander knew that, a few hours after the night battle had ended, the American and British delegations meeting at Ghent had signed a peace treaty, concluding the War of 1812.

✦ ✦ ✦

Keane's inaction following the fight of the 23rd granted Jackson a few additional days to strengthen his position at New Orleans, and to receive reinforcements. He started to improve his location on the canal, which soon became known as the "Line Jackson"—an earthen breastwork extending 600 yards from the Mississippi River across the plain and a further 200 yards into a swamp on the left. Vegetation and many of the buildings fronting it were cleared to create a good field of fire.

On Christmas Day 1814, the new commander of the British land forces arrived in camp. Thirty-two-year-old Edward Pakenham, an Irish-born aristocrat, joined the British Army in 1794, seeing service in the West Indies, where he was wounded, and in Holland. Fighting under his brother-in-law, the Duke of Wellington, in the Peninsular War, he commanded an infantry division and was made Major-General. Considered tactically astute, his bravery on the battlefield endeared him to his officers and men.

On December 28, Pakenham conducted a reconnaissance in force to the American lines using two brigade columns: the right under Major-General Samuel Gibbs, the left under Keane. If possible, he planned to develop it into a full-blown assault on Jackson's position. General Coffee's men stood on the American left where the defenses were far from complete, consisting merely of an abatis reinforced with heaps of earth. Gibbs made good progress, since there was no artillery on his front, and his approach, partially shielded by woods and some plantation buildings, allowed him to outflank the American line. Meanwhile, Keane's men, advancing near the river, joined by some friendly artillery, came under increasing enemy artillery fire from the American works, as well as from a US ship in the Mississippi. He soon put his men under cover in ditches.

Having completed his examination of the American position, and deciding not to attack, Pakenham ordered Keane and Gibbs to withdraw. His conclusion from the action was that Jackson's line could not be turned from its left. Of the decision to retreat when the flanking move was on the verge of success, a British participant at New Orleans (most likely Lieutenant Gleig) called the failure to flank the Americans "contemptible" and that "one spirited dart" would have enabled his comrades to carry the enemy works from "a horde of raw militiamen, ranged behind a mud wall." British casualties for the day numbered 40 to 50 men while the defenders incurred nine killed and nine wounded.

After the British probe of December 28, Jackson accelerated the strengthening of his defenses. On his left he extended the original earthen palisade on the plain—which was at some points 20 feet thick at the base and five feet thick at the top—to the woods with a double rampart of logs, and cleared the ground to its front for 300 yards to provide a good field of fire. At the extreme end of this, he bent the line back to a right angle to provide further protection from a flanking maneuver. Twelve artillery pieces in seven batteries studded the length of his line from the left of the Mississippi, while a three-gun battery, increased to nine guns by January 8, was positioned on the right bank. Jackson also constructed a second defense manned by Louisiana militiamen a mile behind the first with a water-filled ditch in front.

On the foggy morning of January 1, 1815, Pakenham prepared to launch two infantry columns at the "Line Jackson" after his 17 heavy cannon had hopefully suppressed the enemy artillery and breached the American position. The British bombardment continued for three and a half hours against the American line on the left bank of the river, and for another hour against the battery on the right shore. Running low on ammunition, and not appreciably silencing the enemy cannon, Pakenham cancelled the planned infantry assault. Colonel Alexander Dickson, Pakenham's chief of artillery, blamed the ineffectual artillery fire on his "men being so unprotected [from enemy artillery fire], assisted in rendering the fire less active than it otherwise would [have been]."

Pakenham's final attempt to take the Line Jackson took place on January 8. The main attack was to be made on the British right by Gibbs' 2,500-strong 2nd Brigade column, covered by light troops. Soldiers would carry scaling ladders to mount the American parapet, while a contingent of troops would guard the storming force's flank. A secondary attack was to be made by Keane's 1,460-strong 3rd Brigade, with the special mission of capturing the American two-gun redoubt in front of the enemy right. The 1st Brigade, under newly arrived Major-General John Lambert, was placed in the center of the line as a reserve. The general direction of the attack was away from most of the American artillery and toward the left. As a prelude to the main attack, Colonel William Thornton's 780-strong 4th Brigade would cross to the right bank of the Mississippi the night before and take out American positions on that side of the river. He would then be joined by an artillery detachment, which would fire on Jackson's right across the river. Twenty-six pieces of heavy artillery would be available to aid the entire effort against 4,200 Yankee defenders.

Gibbs' men moved out at 4:00am but failed to take the ladders and fascines to fill in the American ditch with them. They had to return to retrieve the material and this cost

British 93rd Highlanders repulsed by US marines during battle of New Orleans. Painting by Charles Waterhouse.

the attackers a half hour of darkness. Worse, the storming parties with the ladders entered the action piecemeal as they raced to the head of Gibbs' column to plant their ladders against the enemy works, many failing to do this after coming under American fire. Thornton's crossing the river was also delayed, adding to the breakdown of Pakenham's plan. The British attack did not commence until 6:00am as dawn broke.

The attempt to take the American redoubt was successful, but the British detachment could not break through the main American position. Meanwhile, Keane veered to his right to support Gibbs with the 93rd Highland Regiment, only to be wounded as the Highlanders "fell like pins in a bowling alley," and, according to Lieutenant Charles Gordon, "after being subjected to a most destructive and murderous fire," which eventually cost the unit 75 percent of its numbers. Gibbs' attack fell apart as his men, without the scaling ladders, desperately tried to claw their way up the parapet from the ditch in front of it. Most were rapidly shot down. Many took shelter in the trench below the mud walls. Above them, sheltered by their earth wall, were "Tennessee riflemen arrayed at the breastwork, the best marksmen in front," according to Lieutenant John Fort, "and the two rear ranks loading and such a blaze of fire was perhaps never seen." Concurring, another militiaman wrote that after the Redcoats managed to move into the ditch, "all the time the deadly rifles of the Americans poured in a steady stream of fire into the British ranks, which soon, riddled through and through, fell back in disorder from the foot of the parapet."

Death of British commander Sir Edward Pakenham at the height of the battle.

General Jackson views the wounded after the battle.

After the signal for the advance was given, Pakenham rode to Gibbs' column. Seeing it stationary and some of the men retreating, he rode to the head of the formation and shouted at them: "For shame, recollect you are British soldiers, this is the road you ought to take." He was persuading the men to move forward again when he was hit in the leg by American grapeshot, killing his horse. Remounted on another steed, he was cheering his troops on when he was struck by a cannon ball that shattered his spine. Around this time, Gibbs also received a fatal wound, and unable to bear the punishment inflicted on them, his 2nd Brigade broke and fled, shortly followed by their supporting artillery.

As their commander lay dying, the 2nd Brigade's light troops, under Lieutenant-Colonel Timothy Jones on the American left, pushed hard against Coffee's 1,200 marksmen, who were "protected by thick bushes, and dealt death from behind them to British platoons whose officers were falling fast but saw no enemy." One such officer was Jones, mortally wounded before his men retreated.

Assuming command of the army after Pakenham's death, Major-General Lambert advanced his 1st Brigade 250 yards away from the American line in order to cover the retreat of the British attacking force and meet any enemy counterattack, which never came. One member of Lambert's Brigade, Sergeant John S Cooper, recalled that as his regiment advanced into position the American firepower was fierce and about "12 files from me on my right [a soldier] was smashed to pieces by a cannon ball." An American soldier described the scene in front of the Line Jackson as one that resembled "a sea of blood," referring to

Blockaded in port for much of the war, USS Constitution *defeated two British warships—* HMS Cyane *and* Levant—*in February 1815.*

the red clad British dead and wounded that covered the battlefield. The time was 8:30am, an hour after the battle had begun, and the contest on the east bank of the river was over.

At the same time, 1,300 yards across the Mississippi River, Brigadier-General David B. Morgan and his 350 Louisiana State Militia were in trouble. Thornton and his British 4th Brigade had finally crossed the river and chased away the militia a mile below the US position. As the British neared Morgan's main defensive line, Thornton described it as "a very formidable redoubt, with the right flank secured by an entrenchment extending back to a thick wood." But there was a gap in its center and the right was exposed, and these Thornton attacked. Kentucky militiamen had arrived to reinforce Morgan, but after a brief firefight they quickly decamped. Entering the main enemy position, the Redcoats captured 12 cannon. Thornton was badly wounded in the assault.

Jackson learned of the reverse to American arms and sent 400 reinforcements over the river to remove the enemy menace. While this was transpiring, Lambert ordered Thornton back to the left bank of the river. After an hour's combat, the battle was over, at a cost to the British of 291 killed, 1,262 wounded and 484 captured or missing. Jackson suffered 13 dead, 39 injured and 19 missing. The vast majority of the British losses were inflicted by American artillery and musket fire. Only 1,200 fabled Kentucky Long Rifles had been present in the fight, spread along Jackson's entire line. By the morning of the 19th, the

British army had withdrawn from the battlefield. By the end of the month, they were on board Cochrane's ships sailing out of the Gulf. On February 12, 1815, 600 troops from Cochrane's fleet took Fort Bowyer in Mobile Bay in preparation to capture Mobile as a base in lieu of New Orleans. The next day, news finally reached the fleet that peace had been made between Great Britain and the United States of America.

✦ ✦ ✦

"If we had either burnt Baltimore or held Plattsburg," wrote Henry Goulburn, member of the British peace delegation meeting with their American counterparts in Ghent, Belgium, on October 21, 1814, "I believe we should have had peace on [our] terms." But the British had not gained either place, and by late 1814 the thought of another costly campaign against the United States in the following year was something His Majesty's Government wished to avoid. For the Americans' part, their nation's inability to successfully carry the war to the enemy in Canada, even with the huge advantage in manpower she possessed, meant that only through a peace treaty could she extricate herself from a financially ruinous and humiliating conflict.

The final form of the peace agreement, which took shape in November 1814, made no mention of the maritime issues that had been the main cause of the conflict in 1812. Both parties would evacuate territories belonging to the other; prisoners were to be quickly exchanged; both would conclude peace accords with the Indians; and disputes over the US-Canadian border would be settled at a future date. The US Senate ratified the Treaty of Ghent on February 15, 1815, and it went into effect on February 17 at 11:00pm.

Of the reasons given for the final settlement, the most sound is that a process of attrition finally exposed the vital national interests both sides harbored. Since there was no single decisive military turning point, and the fundamental positions of the two countries were never that far apart, each was prepared to accept the status quo before the war.

'Home of the brave'—legacy of the War of 1812—extract from Francis Scott Key's lyrics to The Star Spangled Banner, recording the British bombardment of Fort McHenry in 1814 and made the US National Anthem in 1931.

DEFENCE OF FORT M'HENRY.

The annexed song was composed under the following circumstances— A gentleman had left Baltimore, in a flag of truce for the purpose of getting released from the British fleet, a friend of his who had been captured at Marlborough.—He went as far as the mouth of the Patuxent, and was not permitted to return lest the intended attack on Baltimore should be disclosed. He was therefore brought up the Bay to the mouth of the Patapsco, where the flag vessel was kept under the guns of a frigate, and he was compelled to witness the bombardment of Fort M'Henry, which the Admiral had boasted that he would carry in a few hours, and that the city must fall. He watched the flag at the Fort through the whole day with an anxiety that can be better felt than described, until the night prevented him from seeing it. In the night he watched the Bomb Shells, and at early dawn his eye was again greeted by the proudly waving flag of his country.

Tune—ANACREON IN HEAVEN.

O ! say can you see by the dawn's early light,
    What so proudly we hailed at the twilight's last gleaming,
Whose broad stripes and bright stars through the perilous fight,
    O'er the ramparts we watch'd, were so gallantly streaming?
And the Rockets' red glare, the Bombs bursting in air,
Gave proof through the night that our Flag was still there;
    O ! say does that star-spangled Banner yet wave,
    O'er the Land of the free, and the home of the brave?

British Valour and Yankee Boasting or, Shannon versus Chesapeake. Courtesy of the Library of Congress

E BOASTING or, Shannon versus Chesapeake.

British Lion from the quarterdeck of the Macedonian. Courtesy of the Library of Congress

Bibliography

===∞∞∞===

Barbuto, R., *Niagara 1814: America Invades Canada*, Lawrence: University of Kansas Press, 2000.

Barbuto, R., *Long Range Guns, Close Quarter Combat: Third United States Artillery Regiment in the War of 1812*, Youngstown: Old Fort Niagara Association, 2010.

Barbuto, R., "To Prepare an Army: Buffalo 1814," *Military and Naval History Forum* 4 (1996): 27–33.

Berton, P., *The Invasion of Canada, 1812–1813*, Toronto: Anchor Canada, 2002.

Berton, P., *Flames Across the Border: The Canadian-American Tragedy, 1813–1814*, Boston: Little Brown and Company, 1981.

Barney, J., "Letter from Commodore Joshua Barney to the Secretary of the Navy Regarding the Battle of Bladensburg," *Niles Weekly Register*, September 10, 1814.

Blumberg, A., "Quaint British Fireworks: Development and Use of Congreve Rockets during the Napoleonic Wars," *Military and Naval Forum* 1 (1994): 30–39.

Blumberg, A., "Queenston Heights: The Battle that Saved British North America," *Journal of the War of 1812*, Vol 3, #2 (Spring 1998): 5–7.

Blumberg, A., "A Rather Unsuitable Crew: American General Officers at the Start of the War of 1812," *Journal of the War of 1812*, Vol 6, #1 (Winter 2001): 8–10.

Bowler, Arthur, ed., *War Along the Niagara: Essays on the War of 1812 and Its Legacy*, Youngstown: Old Fort Niagara Association, 1991.

Brown, W., *The Amphibious Campaign for West Florida and Louisiana, 1814–1815*, Tuscaloosa: University of Alabama Press, 1969.

Budiansky, S., *Perilous Fight: America's Intrepid Fight with Britain on the High Seas, 1812–1815*, New York: Alfred Knopf, 2011.

Caffrey, K., *The Twilight's Last Gleaming: Britain vs. America, 1812–1815*, New York: Stein and Day, 1977.

Chartrand, R., *British Forces in North America, 1793–1815*, London: Osprey Publishing, 1998.

Courten, A., *Canada 1812–1814: Swiss Regiments*, Bloomington: Trafford Publishing, 2009.

Cress, L., *Citizens in Arms: The Army and the Militia in American Society to the War of 1812*, Chapel Hill: University of North Carolina, 1982.

Cusik, J., *The Other War of 1812: The Patriot's War and the American Invasion of Spanish East Florida*, Gainesville: University Press of Florida, 2003.

Daughan, G., *1812: The Navy's War*, New York: Basic Books, 2011.

Dudley, W., *Splintering the Wooden Wall: The British Blockade of the United States, 1812–1815*, Annapolis: Naval Institute Press, 2003.

Eisenhower, J., *Agent of Destiny: The Life and Times of General Winfield Scott*, New York: The Free Press, 1997.

Elliott, J., *Strange Fatality: The Battle of Stoney Creek 1813*, Toronto: Robin Brass Studio, 2009.

Elting, J., *Amateurs to Arms: A Military History of the War of 1812*, New York: Da Capo Press, 1995.

Eshelman, R., Sheads, S., and Hickey, D., *The War of 1812 in the Chesapeake: A Reference Guide to Historic Sites in Maryland , Virginia, and the District of Columbia*, Baltimore: The Johns Hopkins University Press, 2010.

Everest, A., *The War in the Chaplain Valley*, Syracuse: Syracuse University Press, 1981.

Fitz-Enz, D., *The Final Invasion: Plattsburg, the War of 1812's Most Decisive Battle*, New York: First Cooper Square Press, 2001.

Fortescue, J., *A History of the British Army, Vol 8*, London: MacMillan & Company, 1917.

Fredriksen, J., *War of 1812 Eyewitness Accounts: An Annotated Bibliography*, London: Greenwood Press, 1997.

Fredriksen, J., *Green Coats and Glory: The United States Regiment of Riflemen, 1808–1821*, Youngstown: Old Fort Niagara Publications, 2000.

Fredriksen, J., *The United States Army in the War of 1812: A Concise Biography of Commanders and Operational Histories of Regiments, with Bibliographies of Publications and Primary Sources*, Jefferson: McFarland and Company, 2009.

Fredriksen, J., ed., *The War of 1812 in Person: Fifteen Accounts by United States Army Regulars, Volunteers and Militiamen*, Jefferson: McFarland and Company, 2010.

Fryer, M., *More Battlefields of Canada*, Toronto: Dundurn Press, 1993.

Gardiner, R., ed., *The Naval War of 1812*, Newbury: Chatham Publishing, 1998.

George, C., *Terror on the Chesapeake: The War of 1812 on the Bay*, Shippensburg: White Mane Books, 2000.

Gleig, G., *The Campaigns of the British Army at Washington and New Orleans, 1814–1815*, London: John Murray, 1861.

Graves, D., *Red Coats and Grey Jackets: The Battle of Chippawa, 5 July 1814*, Toronto: Dundurn Press, 1994.

Graves, D., *Where Right and Glory Lead: The Battle of Lundy's Lane, 1814*, Toronto: Robin Brass Studio, 1993.

Graves, D., *Field of Gory: The Battle of Crysler's Farm*, Toronto: Robin Brass Studio, 1999.

Halbert, H., and Ball, T., edited by Owsley, F., *The Creek War of 1813 and 1814*, Tuscaloosa: The University of Alabama Press, 1995.

Hanks, J., Ford, A., and McMullen, A., edited by Graves, D*., Soldiers of 1812: American Enlisted Men's Memoirs of the Niagara Campaign*, Youngstown: Old Fort Niagara Association, 1995.

Hawthorne, N., "A Veteran of the War of 1812 Talks to Nathaniel Hawthorne," *Journal of the War of 1812*, Vol 6, #1 (Winter 2001): 3–6.

Haythornthwaite, P., *Nelson's Navy,* London: Osprey Publishing, 1993.

Haythornthwaite, P., *The Armies of Wellington*, London: Arms and Armour Press, 1994.

Haythornthwaite, P., *British Napoleonic Infantry Tactics, 1792–1815*, Oxford: Osprey Publishing, 2008.

Heidler, D., and Heidler, J., eds., *Encyclopedia of the War of 1812*, Santa Barbara: ABC-CLIO, Inc, 1997.

Henry, C., *British Napoleonic Artillery, 1793–1815: Field Artillery*, Oxford: Osprey Publishing, 2002.

Hickey, D., *The War of 1812: A Forgotten Conflict*, Urbana: University of Illinois Press, 1990.

Hickey, D., *Don't Give Up the Ship*: *Myths* of the War *of 1812*, Champaign: University of Illinois Press, 2006.

Hitsman, J., *The Incredible War of 1812: A Military History*, Toronto: University of Toronto Press, 1965.

Johnson, M., *North American Indian Tribes of the Great Lakes*, Oxford: Osprey Publishing, 2011.

Katcher, P., *The American War, 1812–1814*, London: Osprey Publishing, 1990.

Kemble, C., *The Image of the Army Officer in America*, Westport: Greenwood Press, 1973.

LaRock, J., "The Myth of the Long Rifle: Small Arms at the Battle of New Orleans," *Military and Naval History Forum* 1 (1994): 40–46.

Latimer, J., *1812: War With America*, Cambridge: The Belknap Press of Harvard University Press, 2007.

Lucas, C., *The Canadian War*, Oxford: The Clarendon Press, 1906.

Malcomson, R., *Lords of the Lake: The Naval War on Lake Ontario, 1812–1814*, Annapolis: Naval Institute Press, 1998.

Malcomson, R., *Capital In Flames: The American Attack on York, 1813*, Montreal: Robin Brass Studio, 2008.

Malcomson, R., *The Battle of Queenston Heights*, Canada: Peninsula Press, 1994.

McCranie, K., *Utmost Gallantry: The US and Royal Navies at Sea in the War of 1812*, Annapolis: Naval Institute Press, 2011.

McNab, C., *The Native American Warrior, 1500–1890*, New York: Saint Martin's Press, 2010.

Melish, J., *The Military and Topographical Atlas of the United States Including the British Possessions and Florida*, Philadelphia: John Melish Publishers, 1813.

Muller, C., *The Darkest Day: The Washington-Baltimore Campaign During the War of 1812*, Philadelphia: University of Pennsylvania Press, 2003.

Owsley, F., *Struggle for the Gulf Borderlands: The Creek War and the Battle of New Orleans, 1812–1815*, Gainesville: University Press of Florida, 1981.

Park, S., and Nafziger, G., *The British Military: Its System and Organization, 1803–1815*, Cambridge: Rafm Co, 1983.

Patterson, B., *The Generals: Andrew Jackson and Sir Edward Pakenham, and the Road to the Battle of New Orleans*, New York: New York University Press, 2005.

Peskin, A., *Winfield Scott and the Profession of Arms*, Kent: Kent State University Press, 2003.

Phifer, M., *War of 1812 Along the Upper St. Lawrence River*, Westminster: Heritage Books, 2008.

Pickles, T., *New Orleans 1815*, London: Osprey Publishing, 1993.

Pitch, A., *The Burning of Washington: The British Invasion of 1814*, Annapolis: Naval Institute Press, 1998.

Quimby, R., *The US Army in the War of 1812: An Operational and Command Study*, 2 Vols, East Lansing: Michigan State University Press, 1997.

Reid, S., *British Redcoat, 1793–1815*, London: Osprey Publishing, 1997.

Reid, S., *Redcoat Officer, 1740–1815*, Oxford: Osprey Publishing, 2002.

Reilly, R., *The British at the Gates: The New Orleans Campaign in the War of 1812*, Toronto: Robin Brass Studio, 2002.

Roosevelt, T., *The Naval War of 1812*, Annapolis: Naval Institute Press, 1987 (reprint).

Sheads, Scott, *Fort McHenry*, Baltimore: The Nautical & Aviation Publishing Company of America, 1995.

Shomette, D., *Flotilla: The Patuxent Naval Campaign in the War of 1812*, Baltimore: The Johns Hopkins University Press, 2009.

Skeen, C., *Citizen Soldiers in the War of 1812*, Lexington: The University Press of Kentucky, 1999.

Skaggs, D., and Altoff, G., *A Signal Victory: The Lake Erie Campaign, 1812–1813*, Annapolis, Naval Institute Press, 1997.

Stagg, J., "Soldiers in Peace and War: Comparative Perspective on Recruitment of the United States Army, 1802–1815," *William and Mary Quarterly* 57 (2000): 79–120.

Stanley, G., *Canada's Soldiers, 1604–1954*, Toronto: MacMillan Company of Canada, 1954.

Taylor, A., *The Civil War of 1812*, New York: Alfred Knopf, 2010.

Thompson, J., *Royal Marines: From Sea Soldiers to a Special Force*, London: Pan Books, 2001.

Toll, I., *Six Frigates: The Epic History of the Founding of the US Navy*, New York: W.W. Norton & Company, 2006.

Turner, W., *British Generals in the War of 1812: High Command in the Canadas*, Montreal: McGill-Queens University Press, 1999.

Weigley, R., *The History of the United States Army*, Bloomington: Indiana University Press, 1984.

Whitehorne, J., *While Washington Burned: The Battle for Fort Erie 1814*, Baltimore: The Nautical & Aviation Publishing Company of America, 1992.

Whitehorne, J., *The Battle for Baltimore 1814,* Baltimore: The Nautical & and Aviation Company of America, 1997.

Wilder, P., *The Battle of Sacketts Harbour, 1813,* Baltimore: The Nautical & Aviation Company of America, 1994.

Williams, J., *History of the Invasion and Capture of Washington and the Events which Proceeded and Followed,* New York: Harper & Brothers Publishers, 1857.

Wohler, J., *Charles de Salaberry, Soldier of the Empire, Defender of Quebec,* Toronto: Dundurn Press, 1984.

Zaslow, M., ed, *The Defended Border: Upper Canada and the War of 1812,* Toronto: MacMillan Company of Canada, 1964.

Above: *Victory monument.* Below: *Perry Monument, Canonballs and Guns. Inscription on canonball monument reads:* In Memory Of American and English Heroes Who Fell At Perry's Victory, Sept. 10th, 1813. *Both monuments located in Put-in-Bay Ohio.* Courtesy of the Library of Congress

Index

HMS Shannon *awaiting the close approach of the American frigate* Chesapeake *on June 1, 1813.*
Courtesy of the Library of Congress

"Johnny Bull and the Alexandrians." A cartoon mocking the citizens of Virginia for their lack of resistance to the British in 1814. Courtesy of the Library of Congress

"John Bull making a new Batch of Ships." A satire on British efforts to recover after major naval losses on the Great Lakes in 1813–14. Courtesy of the Library of Congress

P.35   500 Marines